*Observations
on self, family
and life*

RABBI BEREL WEIN

Table of Contents

Preface

1. Stay Disconnected (Sometimes)   1
2. Pass With Caution   5
3. No Bones   9
4. Balance the Weight   13
5. Which Is the Right Key?   17
6. Be Vague   21
7. The Book Cover   25
8. A Family Wall   29
9. What Will They Say About You?   33
10. Buy Green Bananas   37
11. Fools, Nitwits, and Other People You'll Meet   41
12. Don't Grab First   45
13. Wear a Hard Hat   49
14. Invest for the Long Haul   53
15. No Fault? No Way!   57
16. An Amateur Built the Ark, Professionals the Titanic   61
17. Learn to Laugh   65

18.	Don't Count Your Chickens	69
19.	Bridging the Generations	73
20.	Don't Argue, Just Debate	77
21.	Spend Your Grandchildren's Money	81
22.	Count Your Blessings	85
23.	Read and Study History	89
24.	Family Trees	93
25.	You Can't Win Them All	97
26.	The Art of Giving	101
27.	Learn How to Take	105
28.	Good Neighbor Policy	109
29.	Memory's Power and Powerful Memories	113
30.	Clothes Make the Man	119
31.	I Can't or Can't I?	123
32.	Ask for Directions	127
33.	Letting Bygones be Bygone	131
34.	Singin' in the Rain	135
35.	Ruled by the Clock	139
36.	Take the Long Way	143
37.	Can You Keep a Secret?	147
38.	Listening Is More Than Just Hearing	151
39.	Don't Be a Nay-sayer	155
40.	Small Stuff Adds Up	159
41.	It Really Can Be a Good Morning	163
42.	I Am Mad as	167
43.	Don't Argue With the Referee	171

44. Survival Tactics 175
45. But It Is Sooo Boooring! 179
46. Quitters Ultimately Are Losers 183
47. Last Will And Testament 187
48. But I'm not Finished! 191

Preface

I am by nature a person who is loath to interfere in the lives and behavior of others. Therefore, giving advice – and especially unsolicited advice – is very difficult for me. However, the professions that I have followed in my lifetime – lawyer, rabbi, teacher – have always placed me in advice-giving situations. As I became older, I realized that sharing my experiences in life with others was often the most effective advice that I could give to those who asked me for my opinion regarding their personal problems. My advice was not a matter of wisdom as much as it was a sharing of perspectives and life's events – its difficulties and joys. And even though I rarely had hard specific answers to the complex problems that were posed to me, I found that the mere discussion and sharing of experiences appeared to be of benefit and strength to all those concerned.

This book is written in the same vein as those private advice-giving sessions. It may be short on hard specific answers but it is long on perspective and experience.

And I believe that in the long run, perspective and experience eclipse short-term specific answers. This is a book about strategy and not merely tactics. It is meant to reflect attitudes, ideas and principles and not merely rah-rah words of encouragement and unrealistic rosy cheer. There are many bumps on the road of life. This book deals not only with how to swerve around them but also with how to create a suspension frame strong enough to absorb them. The book has no simple answers or easy solutions to life's complexities. But I hope it provides a realistic and even noble framework within which to deal effectively with the adventures of our lives.

I wish to acknowledge the help of the countless hundreds, if not thousands, who over the years have helped me crystallize my thoughts and opinions through their conversations with me. I wish also to thank the staff – all of them now are my friends and colleagues – of Shaar Press for their help and guidance during my writing of this book. My wife, Jackie, has as always been my mainstay and light.

I sincerely hope that this book will awaken ideas and feelings within you, my dear reader, that will be of long term benefit in your life.

Berel Wein

Jerusalem
Kislev 5760 / November 1999

Stay Disconnected (Sometimes)

I n our world of instant and constant communication we are always in touch. Portable phones, e-mail, hard-wired telephones, fax machines, beepers, computers and their other nefarious companions are always vying for our immediate attention. Staying connected and being in touch has become one of the noted tyrannies of modern life. There are times when we all long for the good old disconnected days (at least those of us old enough to remember that there were ever such good old days). Imagine for a moment that no one can reach you, that you are alone, enjoying your privacy, and that the outside world no longer engulfs and dominates you. The serenity occasioned by merely imagining such a situation is pleasurable in itself. Every so often you should guarantee that you will be unreachable for a given period of time. It will do wonders for your nerves and psyche.

I recently read an article in the newspaper written by an American businessman whose firm had stationed him in Tokyo for the last 20 years. He described how in the early years of his association with the company he worked the regular Japanese working day of eight hours and had the evenings and weekends for himself. As the modern technological revolution in communication unfolded, his office in New York began to be in touch with him more and more, and at the working time-clock hours of New York and not only of Tokyo. He wrote that now he is working the equivalent of a 19-hour workday, his weekends are constantly being disrupted, he is not making much more money than he did before, and he is considering leaving his company in order to escape the grind. His story may be extreme but it is not atypical. The company will lose a loyal and experienced employee, he himself will have to cast about to find suitable replacement employment, and his attitude towards work and life itself has probably been permanently impaired. All because in our world one has to always stay in touch!

As a rabbi I always felt that I also had to constantly stay in touch. I ruined most of my family's vacations in my early years as a lawyer by calling my office frequently from wherever we were staying. I was always put in a frustrating and less than cheerful mood by these calls, for they invariably informed me of problems that I could do nothing about then and that would somehow solve themselves anyway by the time I returned to work at my office. When I became a rabbi, I continued with my obsession to constantly remain in touch. It was a matter of religious sacrifice and noblesse oblige that governed me. However, I never was able to truly relax and enjoy a vacation. Finally, I struck a reasonable compromise with my personal self and my perceived rabbinic obligations. Only my trusted secretary knew where I was and she never disturbed me if it were not a matter of true urgency. My final American vacation before moving to Israel was just a wonderful one. No one had my telephone numbers or my itinerary. I was finally disconnected. I cannot describe to you the feeling of freedom and peace that this situation gave me. Try disconnecting for a while yourself. I guarantee that you will enjoy every minute of the freedom it grants you.

Pass With Caution

One of the most lethal causes of road accidents and automobile fatalities is the imprudent passing of cars. Unfortunately, people's impatience overwhelms their common sense. There is no more frightening feeling in the driving experience than being in the left lane, attempting to pass a car at considerable speed, and spying another car coming head-on in that very same lane. Thousands of people are killed yearly because of this penchant to get ahead. Even in city traffic, where the supposed gain usually means arriving at the next red stoplight first, there is an urge within us to pass the car in front – no matter what – that is dangerous and foolish. Good defensive driving habits are necessary in order to mitigate this primitive urge to pass that lurks within all drivers.

This "passing at all costs" behavior is not restricted to automobile driving alone. The urge "to get ahead" is ingrained in the value system of our society. And "getting ahead" often means passing other people who are perceived to be ahead of us. One should be aware of opportunities to get ahead and exploit those situations wisely and gently. But to recklessly crush others who we think are in the way of our own advancement, to pass without caution and without sensitivity towards others, can be disastrous to all concerned. Eventually there is always another car coming towards us in the passing lane and if we are not cautious, judicious and fair in passing, our momentary accomplishment of passing the car/person/position ahead of us may end in tragedy and heartbreak.

The corporate workplace is littered with the skeletons of those who passed without any thought of caution for themselves or concern for others. Life and literature are full of the stories of those who successfully climbed the ladder of success, ruthlessly passing others on the way, pushing them off the ladder, and yet eventually being toppled themselves. They finally encountered the other car coming towards them in the passing lane and discovered that they had no more mobility or space left to swerve out of harm's way. Passing with caution is therefore not just a matter of courtesy and good sense. It is a guarantee of getting to one's goal safely and being able to remain there and enjoy the accomplishment.

In a harsh and very competitive world, the temptation to overtake and pass – even in a morally aggressive and physically unsafe, unwarranted manner – is quite tempting. It takes great strength of character and moral conscience – as well as just plain, good old common sense – to refrain from doing so. Yet, not restraining ourselves can cause us eventual disaster and end our dreams and goals. We, too, become affected by our negative actions.

Passing on the road is usually a split-second decision, not invested with much planning or strategic thinking. Passing in life and in careers, on the other hand, is for the most part a planned component of a longer and well-thought-out process. Passing imprudently and without proper caution on the road can result in instant injury or even death. Passing in life is potentially just as lethal, albeit with longer reaction and processing time. One can lull oneself into thinking that there are no cars approaching in the passing lane, but one must always be aware that beyond the curve or over the rise lurks great potential danger. So pass only with caution, both on the road and in life.

No Bones

My wife has a special recipe for the hot dish of stew meat, potatoes and beans (commonly known as *cholent* to Jews of Eastern European extraction) that is the centerpiece of our Sabbath lunch meal. It is enormously fattening and wickedly delicious. But on the holy Sabbath we are protected from the ravages of otherwise less than healthy foods. And therefore I have enjoyed this delicacy without compunction for more than 40 years of happily married life. When we lived in the United States, where there never is a shortage of meat, one of the recipe ingredients that weekly went into the great stew pot were marrow bones. When we moved to Jerusalem, we discovered that meat, though certainly available there, is not nearly as plentiful as it is in the United States. Not only that, but to our greater chagrin, we discovered that marrow bones are available only in a sporadic and uncertain pattern. We were so persistent in our pursuit of bones that our friendly local butcher, when he would meet me on the street, no longer said, "Good morning," but instead muttered, "No bones yet." So we had to become accustomed to our favorite dish of the week no longer always containing marrow bones.

My wife, in her ingenuity and creativity, discovered substitutes for the marrow bones, so that the taste of this hot dish was restored to its original prize-winning level. When the butcher passes me in the street and says, "No bones yet," I give him a cheerful smile and a hearty, "Good day." We have overcome the marrow bones problem. We have found the available substitute for that savory dish's missing ingredient. No bones does not mean no *cholent*. It merely means different ingredients to create the new *cholent*.

Of all the traits in life that are truly admirable, I have always felt that resiliency, flexibility, and adaptability are the ones to treasure most. There are many occasions in life when we end up in a "no bones" situation. What we do about that situation is the true test of our mettle in life. Many people may just give up when there are no bones and stop preparing *cholent*. But the wise and hardy person will contrive his or her *cholent* even without having marrow bones. There are many situations that are irreversible; sadly, there are many serious and depressing "no bones" periods in everyone's lifetime, but the ability to deal with these occurrences is one of the true tests that we all must face.

One day when I was walking down the street I met our butcher. With a wicked gleam in his eye, he said to me, "I have bones for you today!" I hastened home to tell my wife this momentously good news. Now we were faced with a terrible dilemma. Should we take the marrow bones and run the risk of almost certain disappointment in the future when there would be no bones, or should we take advantage of their present availability? This is always a great problem in life. We took the bones, had a great *cholent* that Sabbath and enjoyed it fully. We were aware of the fact that there would be a day of "no bones" as well, but since by necessity we had developed an answer to the "no bones" problem, we were able to smack our lips over the wonderful marrow bones that came our way. I think that this is a great formula for living life in general, not only for marrow bones and *cholent*.

Balance the Weight

I n Israel, where I now reside, it is common for people to carry their groceries home from the store/supermarket rather than having their orders delivered. The streets are very narrow in all of the major cities, parking is always at a premium, and driving is a special hassle; therefore, people walk. Now the groceries come in thin plastic bags with handles that allow the customer to carry more than one bag in each hand at one and the same time. In order to be able to successfully carry a number of bags of groceries in each hand for the requisite number of blocks until reaching one's home, the bags must be evenly weighted. If one arm is forced to carry a disproportionate share of the weight, the walk home will be most uncomfortable, if not downright disastrous. As in all else in life, balance is the key ingredient to achieving success in transporting heavy grocery bags to one's home.

Balance is necessary in all areas of human life and endeavor. Problems always abound and successful living means learning how to balance them. There are instances in a family when there is a problem with one of the children. Unfortunately in many cases, the whole family is disrupted if not destroyed by the problem of one of its members. It is as though the healthy and well-adjusted are to be sacrificed on the altar of the sick and the troubled. There is no sense of balance regarding the other children in the family that could prevent the problem with one from becoming disaster for all. One must learn how to carry life's problems with equal balance, isolate them and not allow them to unbalance the entire structure of family and social life.

There is an ancient Jewish fable about a man who was embarking on a ship, and he was carrying two very heavy suitcases. There were no porters available so he had to lug those heavy suitcases up the gangplank and onto the ship on his own. His friend, departing on the same ship, asked him what was in those suitcases. The man replied that one contained precious documents, diamonds and money while the other suitcase was filled with rocks. "Why do you need a suitcase of rocks?" he was asked. "In order to balance the weight while I am carrying the heavy suitcase filled with valuables," was the man's reply. "Well, my foolish friend, you could have taken two smaller suitcases and filled each with your valuables and thus have maintained balance without dragging along worthless rocks," was the other man's retort. On the sea journey a great storm arose and the captain of the ship realized that in order to save his vessel and its passengers he would have to lighten the load. The captain ordered all of the passengers to immediately dump overboard half of the suitcases and belongings that they had brought on board. As his friend sheepishly looked on, the man gleefully threw his suitcase of rocks overboard, retaining his entire treasure for himself.

The moral of the story is that in life one must not only carry burdens in a balanced fashion, but also in a way that if circumstances so require, one can cast away certain burdens and property in order to save those other things that are of true and lasting value. Therefore, one must pack carefully and wisely for life's journey, while always making sure that the weights carried in life are properly balanced.

Which Is the Right Key?

I don't know why I have so many keys on my key chain. I am certain that each and every one of them is quite important and vitally necessary for me to carry. Otherwise, they would not be on my key chain, right? But often, when I take out my key chain for actual use, I am dismayed by the array of keys that are on it. I have not the faintest idea which doors many of those keys are supposed to open. The vast number of keys that I have on my key chain, coupled with my failing memory and physical clumsiness, decrees that I always have to try quite a number of keys before I finally find the right one. I long ago attempted to solve this problem by color coding my keys but I am not too adept at recalling which color goes with which door, and in any event I have far more keys than there are colors. So, I have resigned myself to the tried and true, always foolproof method of discovering which key opens the door – namely, trial and error (usually a lot of error).

All of us have many keys on our key chain of life. There are some (not many) master keys which can be used over and over again to unlock doors which life and circumstances have slammed shut in our faces. But then there are particular, sometimes even just one-time-use keys, which can be used to open the locked doors of our problems and challenges. The trick is to know which key to use to open which door. And just as is the case with my overloaded key chain, a great deal of trial and error methodology is involved until one gets the right door open in life's real circumstances. One should therefore always identify the few passkeys that one possesses – patience, serenity, modesty, self-control – and then proceed to identify the other keys which work in certain situations but not in all. Identifying those keys and those situations then becomes the method of successful problem solving and living. One should never give up on the trial and error method. It is the default position in life and allows us all a fail-safe mechanism to open the necessary doors we need to enter.

In life every individual whom we meet and with whom we interact is a different and new door that we have to unlock. In almost all instances we have on our key chain the ideal key to accomplish this. But initially we may not be able to find the right key for this particular door/lock/person. We should not persist and try to force the wrong key into the lock. This will only create frustration, anger, and the feeling of depression and sadness. Instead we should fiddle with our imaginary key chain and keep on trying to find the right key that somehow fits this particular lock.

However, there are limits to searching for the right key. We must remember that there are certain locks for which we do not have any key. There are people and situations that are never amenable to rational solutions. Then we have to learn how to live in a world that will always have locked doors and inadequate key chains. If after due trial and error we discover such a situation/problem/person we should be content with letting that door remain locked, as we move on to the other doors in life for which we do have the right key.

Be Vague

One of the outstanding – in fact, defining – features of politicians the world over is their unfailing ability to be vague. They are masters at obfuscation (this word itself is an example of the meaning of obfuscation) and champions at being decidedly and definitely ambiguous. They justify this seemingly unworthy behavior on grounds ranging from the more noble one of "national security" to the more believable one of just plain old ignorance. In spite of this bad example set for us by our political leaders, I believe that being vague has a time and place in the conduct of our life's affairs. Very rarely in life do we encounter clear-cut "yes or no" issues. Most of life is gray, in-between, ambivalent and shrouded in doubt and uncertainty. As such, it is only natural that frequently the only proper response to the questions asked of us is vagueness. In fact, often the vague answer is the only truly honest one.

The ability to respond "I don't know" or "I am not sure" to questions and problems that life or individuals pose is the hallmark of true intellectual and human honesty. I am skeptical about people who know everything and always have an answer. The great Biblical and Talmudic commentator, Rabbi Shlomo Itzchaki (Rashi), often states in his works, "I do not know the meaning of this word or phrase." Well, if he doesn't know the meaning of the word or phrase why doesn't he just ignore it? Of what purpose is his stating that he doesn't know the correct meaning? I have always felt that his purpose in including in his commentary the admission that "I don't know…" is an enormous educational lesson for life and true scholarship. Otherwise, we, the students of his commentary, would have assumed that the word or phrase in the Bible or Talmud is so simple and self-understood that it requires no comment. Rashi alerts us to the fact that just the opposite is true. He is teaching us that this is an obscure and difficult phrase or word and will require great effort on the part of the reader/student to interpret it. "I don't know" or "I am not at all sure of the answer" are the phrases that often are the most illuminating.

Yet life and living require definitive answers. Some answers may be postponed, but to most questions and problems, eventual answers must be forthcoming. The blessing of vagueness is then a diluted one. Even when one answers definitively, the blessing of vagueness should not be forgotten. A person always has to be open to say that "I have made a mistake" or that "I made the wrong decision." We thus operate on somewhat contradictory paths in our lives. We act upon our decisions in a forthright manner as though we are completely convinced of their correctness. And yet, there always remains within us a small voice that nags at us and says, "Maybe, you were not right." That small voice is essential for successful living. It allows us to turn around before it is too late, to analyze our decisions honestly, and to continually grow and mature spiritually and emotionally. Even when we are certain of things, we should always leave room within our hearts and minds for a little vagueness.

The Book Cover

publisher friend of mine told me long ago that anyone who says that "you can't tell (or sell) a book by
its cover" is obviously not in the book business.
The truth of the matter is that a book cover does matter,
and external appearance does play a role in most areas
of human endeavor. The truly sophisticated and sensitive
person may pride himself on being able to ignore the
cover and deal only with the content of the book. The
great Rabbi Meir cautioned us not to judge the quality of
the wine by the appearance of the bottle in which it is
contained. But all of us are well aware that the beauty
and shape of the bottle can certainly attract the buyer
and help sell the wine. And conversely, an unattractive
bottle is unlikely to draw people to taste the wine that it
holds. Therefore, the rabbis of the Talmud cautioned the
scholars and students of Torah to appear neatly dressed

and cleanly garbed. Over the centuries, poverty, persecution, and the circumstances of exile all combined to dim the light of this message to many, but its inherent truth should be plain for all to see in today's world.

"Clothes make the man" was the slogan of Victorian England. An overemphasis on the importance of this statement can lead to foppish dress and self-indulgence, as it indeed did in many cases. But there is no doubt that clothes do say something about the person wearing them. Now, it may well be that what clothes say about us is misleading or even untrue. Jewish tradition somehow always portrays the immortal prophet Elijah as wearing tatters. Yet that certainly is not representative of the man, his influence and his mission. Rightly or wrongly, people judge us by our appearance, our cleanliness, the shine (or lack of shine) of our shoes and the neatness of our overall demeanor. There are times in life to "dress up" and times to "dress down," but neatness and good appearance are almost always a requirement.

The importance of presenting a proper appearance should never be minimized. A judge who does not wear a judicial robe in court somehow gives the impression of being insufficiently judicial. Similarly, a doctor who dresses casually and does not wear a white coat weakens our confidence in his or her medical abilities. While we all know that these reactions on our part are nonsensical, nevertheless they are very real reactions.

Caring about personal appearance is an excellent habit. It teaches one respect for oneself and for others as well. It provides a proper framework for our social talents. It is the beautiful binding of the books of our lives. It sets the stage for us to fulfill the nobility of purpose for which we were created. So remember to always put a nice cover on your life's book.

A Family Wall

have written elsewhere on this subject in one of the small essays that make up this book (see "Family Trees"), but I run the risk of repeating myself in this essay because I wish to view the subject from a slightly different angle. And, anyway, repetition of good ideas only strengthens their impact. Finally, I liked both articles so much that I could not part with either one. So, please excuse the redundancy and read on.

One of the greatest accomplishments in life is being able to pass on to the new generation the images, experiences and memories of the older generation. However, in our urbanized, mobile and essentially rootless society, family members of the same generation find it difficult to bond together, let alone to unite different generations of the same family. All of us should have some idea of our ancestors and our family's roots. What did they look like? Where did they live? Why did they or didn't they emigrate from the countries of their birth? What did they do for a living? What is special about their lives and about our family? Knowing the answers to these questions and realizing where we come from, so to speak, helps place us in some perspective of time and circumstance. And perspective is the key to successful living and inner self-worth.

In our home in Jerusalem we have a long corridor that leads from the living/dining area of the apartment to the sleeping/working section of the home. On the long bare wall that forms one side of this corridor, my wife and I have created a "family wall." On that wall are pictures of five generations of our family. Our grandparents, parents, siblings, uncles, aunts, children and grandchildren are all united on this wall. Some of the pictures date back eight decades. The backgrounds for the photographs are Lithuania and Chicago, British-Mandate Palestine and modern-day Israel, Indiana and New York State. There is a wedding-day photograph of my wife's father and mother taken in front of the ramshackle wooden hut of my wife's grandfather in Vaskaaii, Lithuania. Many of our children and grandchildren, nieces and nephews, strikingly carry my mother-in-law's beauty on their faces. There is a class photograph of the students attending a great yeshivah in Jerusalem taken over 75 years ago. And there is my father in the second row of the picture, wearing his fedora at a rakish angle. Our 18-year-old grandson, now attending a great Jerusalem yeshivah as well, looks exactly like him. My mother's engagement picture is there on our wall. And there is a picture, taken from the front page of the December 8, 1925 Kansas City Journal, showing my grandfather, in full rabbinic attire (cane and all) arriving in Kansas City for a session of a special rabbinic court hearing. There is another picture of my grandfather teaching his Talmud class at the Chicago Yeshivah in the early 1940s. He is holding a magnifying glass in his hand, for cataracts had slowly dimmed his eyesight, but it is clearly apparent from the angle of his head that this condition had certainly not dimmed his spirit. My uncles and aunts who arrived in the Holy Land in the early 1930s and were pioneers there in the field of the rabbinate and education, also peer down from our family wall. There is a picture of my wife and me with the President of the State of Israel on the occasion of our dedicating a volume of the Encyclopedia Talmudit. And there are many pictures of Bar and Bat Mitzvah-age grandchildren with their shining faces that look out on the future of our family from our "family wall."

Whenever our younger grandchildren visit us, we always give them a guided, explanatory tour of our "family wall." I have found this experience to be one of the most satisfying of all of the joys of grandparenting. We have encouraged them at an early age to make certain that they will also have a "family wall" in their homes. They have solemnly assured us that they will do so. With such a "family wall" in my grandchildren's home, I am hopefully sanguine about our family's future as a whole unit, interconnected and blessed with historic and spiritual perspective.

What Will They Say About You?

As all of us who have attended funerals know, eulogies vary widely in quality of content, excellence of delivery, and accurate portrayal of the deceased. Even Jewish tradition, which is always a stickler for honesty and truth, allows for some positive exaggeration in the description of the deceased's life and activities during the delivery of a eulogy. Because of this trend, there are many people who leave instructions disallowing any eulogies at all at their inevitable funeral. Better truthful silence than banal and less than truthful compliments, is how they see it. And the purpose of the eulogy, when it does take place, should be to inspire and move the living listeners and not to please the dead subject of the eulogy.

What if we were to write our own eulogy before our death? What would we dare say about ourselves? What traits would we publicly boast about? Would we say, "I was a hard-nosed businessman"? Or, "I was an acquisitive, greedy person who placed money as my highest priority in life"? Or, "I was a very difficult spouse/parent/boss/employee/co-worker/partner"? Or would we say, "I always had to have my way, no matter what or who was in the way"? I don't think that any of the above descriptive phrases would satisfy us as a fitting eulogy for ourselves. But if any of the above is a true description of ourselves, then why shouldn't it be our eulogy? The truth is that throughout our lives we are constantly writing and rewriting our eventual eulogy, even if we are not consciously aware of doing so. Perhaps not the formal, public and exaggeration-prone one the clergyman will intone over us, but rather the true and telling one that our families and acquaintances will silently construct in their hearts and minds and souls. And certainly in the last analysis, that is the only eulogy that really counts. And that silent eulogy and heartfelt appraisal will be remembered long after the public and formal one is forgotten.

In illustration of the above, may I tell you the following story: A distinguished, but very tough negotiator, lawyer friend of mine rose to communal prominence. One day, he was visiting the editor of the local newspaper in his office. The editor said to him, "How would you like to read your own obituary? We have everyone of prominence in our obituary files and we periodically update the general obituary with new details." My friend agreed to read his own obituary. He was shocked and saddened to see that the whole tone of the obituary emphasized what a tough and unyielding person he was. That may have been how he practiced law, but it was not the way he wanted to be eternally remembered. After that incident he changed his attitude towards negotiations and people. By the way, he was no less successful in his law practice thereafter.

I realize that thoughts of eulogies are generally depressing. Nevertheless, they need not be if we are able to focus on the true meaning of our lives. In essence, whenever we do or say something, we should be asking ourselves, "Is this how I want to be remembered?" By posing that question to ourselves on an ongoing and regular basis we would automatically become better people and live happier, less strife-torn lives. Life would therefore have greater meaning and dimension for us, and we would treasure it more dearly and live it more enthusiastically. So thinking about our own eulogy is not necessarily sad or negative. Rather it is like a spice that enhances the flavor of the food that we serve and eat. It lends reality and perspective to our attitudes and actions. It disciplines our speech and behavior and it can help save us from making dangerous and crippling mistakes in our lives. In reality, we should be grateful that we have the opportunity to write, rewrite and improve upon our eulogy while we are yet alive. We can thereby actually shape our own destiny and define how we will be remembered. So, write on and keep improving!

Buy Green Bananas

The morbid "black humor" advice given older people is: "Don't buy green bananas." However, following such advice is self-defeating and self-confirming. Numerous geriatric surveys and studies have shown that older people who have definite plans and goals in mind for their future live longer and healthier lives that those who just sit around and patiently wait out their days. One must always have a goal in mind. People look forward to a family wedding, a birth or an anniversary, the completion of a book or a degree, or traveling on a cruise or a trip. Somehow the human mind is strong enough to allow us to will ourselves to continue to live. By having definite goals in our mind and heart, even if those goals appear initially to be far distant in time, we are able to add resources to our mental strength, and length to our years. Activity, mental and physical, is the key to productive longevity.

Having such future long-range goals changes the definition of the elusive term "quality of life" used by so many people today. I have never understood how one human being can judge another human being's "quality of life." I feel that any reasoning person will be aware that there are truly no objective standards for measuring the desire to continue living, even under apparently difficult, painful and trying circumstances. There are situations when people suffer crippling disease and horrendous pain. To the healthy observer, the sufferer would certainly now prefer death because of the very poor "quality of life" remaining for him or her. However, a rabbi friend of mine told me of visiting a terminally ill patient, a Holocaust survivor, who constantly needed strong sedatives because of the painful nature of his sickness. The man became lucid for a few moments and recognized his rabbi sitting at the side of the bed. He whispered to the rabbi, "Tell the doctors to keep me alive as long as they can. My granddaughter is going to give birth any day now, and I want to live to have a great-grandchild!" For this patient, "quality of life" no longer had anything to do with pain or sedation. Rather, the only issue involved was living long enough to know that he was now a great-grandfather.

There is also a sense of reward and accomplishment

present when one works on a project knowing full well that he or she will not be around for the completion of that project. Realizing that what we do and accomplish will live on after us affords us a tangible sense of immortality. Above all else is the knowledge that we will be remembered. The rabbis of the Mishnah phrased it well when they said: "It is not incumbent upon you to complete the tasks. But neither are you free to withdraw from those tasks." This rule applies to us at all stages of life. Schubert's "Unfinished Symphony" is perhaps his greatest piece of musical composition. So keep on planning, working, and accomplishing. And if there is a good buy on green bananas go right ahead and purchase them, and be fully confident that you will be around long enough to enjoy them.

Fools, Nitwits,
and Other People You'll Meet

One of the most difficult tasks in interpersonal relationships is dealing with people who are fools. Scott Adams has made a deserved fortune with his Dilbert character detailing the foolish foibles of corporate America. But fools are not restricted to the management of corporations or the bureaucracy of government. They abound everywhere, and many times, nay, even most times, are otherwise fine decent people. But they just don't get it! And because of that mentally fatal flaw in their makeup, they make life more difficult for the rest of us wise people who do get it. Having a fool for a boss, a client, an employee, a relative, or worst of all, an adversary, guarantees problems, troubles, frustration and real pain. But since fools and nitwits are always part of society, the wise must develop strategems to deal with them and the situations they cause.

Firstly, every human being is deserving of being dealt with kindly and respectfully. Insulting and demeaning other people is never a successful strategy for solving life's social problems, even though the urge to do so may be irresistible. So a great deal of self-control is necessary in dealing with the fools amongst us. One has to prepare oneself for every such encounter and always strive never to be caught unawares by a chance meeting with someone known to you as being a fool. The ideal strategy is to have as little as possible to do with that person. Of course when that person is your immediate superior at work or your wealthiest law client, this piece of sound advice becomes difficult to follow. Nevertheless, avoidance of fools and nitwits is always a good tactic and should be implemented to the greatest extent possible.

If you have to deal with such people, patience, a sense of humor and silence are necessary components in your arsenal. Always remember that a fool is unaware of the fact that he or she is a fool. Thus arguing logically – or even worse emotionally – is counter-productive to your goal of disengaging as quickly and as easily as possible from the situation. Noncommittal agreement, nodding heads and vague generalities are always valuable in conversations with fools and nitwits. Realize that the person who is talking to you is unaware that he is a fool and thus confronting him with that fact will result in an enormously unpleasant experience. Some of us are able to tolerate fools more gladly than others. Yet all of us must learn to deal more patiently with the challenges that their presence amongst us constantly presents.

My long experience in law and the rabbinate has taught me that one should not allow fools to prattle on endlessly in their conversations with you. You must always develop an escape hatch, contrived or real, that will extricate you from the situation after a reasonable amount of time has passed. Always provide yourself with a seemingly legitimate excuse to leave, and thus end the conversation. Never allow yourself to be trapped with a fool for an indefinite time. Such a scenario will be harmful to your health. If all else fails, my friends, then hand him or her this article in this book which you were wise enough to buy and read. I guarantee results!

Don't Grab First

I was once present at a wedding reception where there were tables of food groaning from their weight and variety. For the most part, the invited guests were attacking the food in frenzied abandon. In the midst of the food orgy, the waiters brought in additional foods of greater quality and uniqueness. A collective groan arose from those already gorging themselves at the tables. Their reaction to the new food being brought out was: "We are already full! We had no idea that these delicacies were yet to be served. We feel cheated!" I then remembered a lesson taught to me by a teacher I had in my early childhood days. He said, "Don't grab first!" By that he meant that one should always consider future possibilities and make reasoned inquiries before jumping to conclusions, making decisions or even eating at a smorgasbord table. The tendency to grab first is born within us of the fear that somehow we will miss out on the opportunity before us at this moment. It exhibits a lack of patience and foresight, a fatal but all too common weakness to settle for the short-term minimum gain and forsake the opportunity to realize the long-term maximum profit.

This rule – "Don't grab first" – applies to almost every facet of human existence. It certainly pertains in the business world where the adage of "timing is everything" rules supreme. But it is equally valuable as a rule of life in many other areas of human behavior. Advertising and publicity, slick marketing techniques and our own personal weaknesses drive us to grab first. Impulse buying is the name of the game in stores and supermarkets throughout the world. The wise customer, the sensible shopper, will always resist the impulse to grab first. Careful consideration of events and circumstances and an awareness that things may not really be as they seem to be are the necessary tools for wise decisions in life.

Of course, we are always subject to our own emotions and perceived needs, as well as to the true necessities of the moment. A thirsty person in the desert should not pass up an oasis that is nearby in hopes of finding a more luxuriant one later on. If someone "just has to have" the item being displayed in the store, that person will undoubtedly purchase it. But generally speaking the rule of "Don't grab first" is a good and intelligent one. Job offers, business ventures, choices of schools and careers, not to mention choices in human relationships, should not be made hastily or impulsively. The fallout from bad decisions too quickly arrived at is many times catastrophic. We are all aware that basic decisions must be made within time constraints. But those time constraints should not be allowed to force us into unwise agreements and foolish actions. The mature and intelligent individual will weigh many factors before making basic decisions and commitments. Rarely, if ever, do we regret actions and behavior that we did not do. Words never spoken need never be apologized for. Life requires us to be enthusiastic and bold. But it does not demand of us unthinking actions or incautious behavior. Rather, we are constantly taught by our experiences in life the truth and practicality of following the rule – "Don't grab first."

Wear a Hard Hat

All of us are familiar with the sign seen at construction sites around the world stating that entry to the site is strictly forbidden unless one is wearing a hard hat. Because of the ubiquitous nature of this sign, construction workers generally and those working on steel superstructures particularly have become known as "hard-hats." But the truth is that all human beings have to wear a hard hat in every phase of their life's endeavors. All of us are constantly being harassed and annoyed by nitpicking critics who cast stones – or nuts and bolts – at our projects, dreams, aspirations and goals. To survive this inevitable onslaught, one needs to wear a hard hat. A hard hat need not be a symbol of stubbornness. It is certainly, however, a symbol of tenacity and personal independence. It allows the depressing comments and dire predictions of others to bounce off our head instead of entering our mind and becoming a part of our personality and psyche. One will rarely be able to achieve anything of creative worth in life if one does not wear a hard hat.

In my own personal life, I recall that before almost every project or position in employment that I have ever undertaken, well-meaning "friends" discouraged me from going forward. Every possible problem and pitfall was outlined for me. Now many of those problems actually did arise when I began the project or work. But none of them justified the abandoning of the project and work position. There never is a problem-free environment or project. I remember that after a particularly difficult and problem-laden day of work, one of my associates complained about the presence and difficulty of those problems. I pointed out to him that if it were not for the presence of those problems none of us would have our jobs. We were hired specifically to deal with the ever-present problems of that field of endeavor. In order to excel at whatever one does, a person requires tenacity of purpose, creativity of ideas, optimism and a quality hard hat on his or her head.

Wearing a hard hat is particularly necessary for people who are of "minority" religious, racial or ethnic background. They are automatically subjected to having the debris of the then-prevailing majority culture dumped on their heads. The struggle to retain one's own deeply held beliefs, traditions, value system and lifestyle – when these are at variance with the majority culture of the surrounding environment – is truly a monumental one. Though the "melting pot" theory of nationalism has faded in the latter third of our century, it is still a daunting task to be proudly different in any society, no matter how free and democratic it may be. A hard hat protects against the comments, looks and slurs that are unavoidable when one is perceived as being purposely different. A hard hat becomes the garment of one's self-worth and self-confidence. It does not and cannot and should not shut out the rest of the world. But it does allow the wearer to be himself or herself and to pursue those goals in life that are most dear to him or her. I think that our world needs more hard-hatters. Being one of those hard-hatters would make life more interesting, if not even more rewarding and satisfying.

Invest for the Long Haul

All financial planners and investment counselors preach one basic lesson repeatedly and insistently: "Invest for the long haul." Do not panic if there are no instant major returns and gains, we are always told. Even if there are temporary setbacks and apparent paper losses, stick with your investment plan, we are again advised. History has shown that over the space of years or decades the investment portfolio will rise in price and appreciate in value. Therefore, to be successful in this financial venture, one should begin investing early in life and be prepared to hold the course for many years. This is sound investment advice, or at least it has been proven to be so over the last 70 years of the American and global economy. Though all financial advice ends with the caveat that "past performance is no guarantee of future results," it is apparently safe to say that investing for the long haul instead of the quick buck is really good financial advice.

But investing for the long haul is not only good financial advice. It is essentially a way of life and a vision of one's goals and self. Our current society is one of impatience and the constant necessity for instant gratification; therefore the long haul holds precious little attraction for many of us. Yet, a life of "now," with the pursuit of short-term benefits and pleasures, usually is counter-productive to the achievement of worthy lifetime goals. It results in opportunistic instead of strategically sound decisions, poor marriages and ravaged families, and a general feeling of vague dissatisfaction with whatever we possess or do. Much of the blame for the mental depression that afflicts so many in today's Western society is directly attributable to the lack of long-term goals and the prevalence of short-term pleasures. We have substituted tactics for strategy, pleasure for achievement. And deep within us there is a part of our being that is very unhappy with this situation.

All of the worthwhile things in life – family, career, education, wisdom and maturity – require a long-range plan and focus. Not only what is good for my child at age 5, but what is good for my child for all of his or her adult life is what should guide parents' decisions regarding their children. Anyone who engages in a regular exercise regimen knows that short-term pain can nevertheless bring great long-term gain. Proper hygiene and diet, avoidance of dangerously unhealthful substances and habits, all are necessary for continued good health. Our society is witness to tens of millions of people who, even though knowing better, persist in short-term pleasures which can significantly curtail the quality and length of their lives. This only shows how pernicious the attraction of the short-term over the long-term really is. For long-term gain always presupposes the willingness of individuals to sacrifice, to do with less, to inhibit their desires and passions. That type of sacrifice is not popular but it is vitally necessary for ultimate success in life. It is our investment for the long haul in our future and in ourselves. Long-term goals provide us with an anchor to hold onto in times of dramatic change and turmoil. The best investment that we can make in life is in ourselves – in our deeply held hopes and aspirations. This wise investment is worthwhile only if made for the long haul.

No Fault? No Way!

We live in a no-fault world. From auto insurance policies to domestic relations court, the prevailing attitude is that no one is really at fault. The lack of accountability has become a hallmark of our century. Eichmann said that he was only following orders, and therefore the murder of millions becomes somehow excusable. Schools regularly advance failing students to higher grades, thus teaching the lesson that accomplishment does not really matter and that no one is truly held accountable for unacceptable performance or behavior. Even in the marketplace and in commercial life, mistakes often go unpenalized and no one person assumes responsibility for mishaps and negligence. "It's not my fault" is the prevailing motto for millions in our society today. Such an attitude is lethal for the individual and for society as a whole.

It is important that children be trained while young in the discipline of responsibility and accountability. The basis of all religious faith is the notion that human beings are held responsible and accountable for their individual behavior, accomplishments and failures. The home that does not instill this basic value in its children does them a great disservice. Accountability need not be taught through punishment or frowns. It can and should be taught through love, corrections, tutoring, training and – most importantly – by personal example. But it must be taught. For otherwise we raise a generation of anything-goes, who-cares and so-what people. The mere thought of having to live in such a wild world should be sobering enough to make us realize the necessity and centrality of accountability in our everyday working and family lives. The necessity for reinforcing this idea of accountability is even greater in a society that shies away from enforcing standards and norms of behavior or performance. The society or family that attempts to function without the acceptance of personal accountability rapidly becomes the lawless society, the woeful family.

Assigning useful chores and projects to children to fulfill as part of their roles as members of the household is an excellent way to instill the lessons of responsibility in them. At first they will probably not be willing participants in the venture, but parents have to persevere with patient firmness. I recall that when my children were growing up, I assigned them the task of taking the full trash bags out to the garbage collection bin in back of our house. I explained to them that performing such a task should be viewed as an honor and not as pure drudgery. I mentioned that in the Temple in Jerusalem the priests actually drew lots to determine who would have the honor of removing the previous day's ashes and garbage from the Holy Altar. They all listened solemnly to my explanation and I felt that I had made my point. However, the next day they came and told me that since the removal of the garbage from the house was such an honor, they wanted me, as the father of the house, to have that honor! Eventually, I was able to persuade them that this should be their contribution to the smooth functioning of our household. But, more importantly, I think that they absorbed the message of responsibility and accountability that came along with the specific chore. There is no greater gift than this that parents can give to their children.

An Amateur Built the Ark, Professionals the Titanic

This brilliant little essay is inspired by a blurb I saw recently in an e-mail communication that I received. Those pithy little sentences read: "Never be afraid to try something new. Remember, an amateur built the ark. Professionals built the Titanic." There are innate tendencies within us that work at cross-purposes with one another. On one hand, there exists within all of us the great fear of the unknown. Newton's law of inertia holds true not only in the mechanical and physical world of physics but in the world of human psychology and spirit as well. People crave security and therefore remain in jobs, relationships and situations which are unsatisfying, simply because they fear the uncertainty of change. On the other hand, human beings possess an inner drive to explore the unknown, to discover the secret and hidden, to risk and be an adventurer. All human progress in science, commerce, navigation, mechanics and even government stems from this latter drive – from the spirit of bold adventure that always nudges us to try something new.

Observe an infant at play, crawling on the floor. An infant is really an unlearned and uninhibited adult human being. The infant will reach for anything on the floor, will tirelessly examine its environment and will wail and complain when well-meaning adults thwart its attempts at discovery and change. This is the natural state of human beings – inquisitive, adventurous, never at rest, always looking to tinker and improve. In our always-uncertain world it is natural to crave security and stability. Financial planners, estate planners, insurance experts and politicians in office all attempt to convince us that the way it is now is how it will be in the future as well. However, all of us in our secret hearts know that the only thing certain about the future is that it will not be the same as the present. Therefore, we should be prepared to be open to new circumstances, to a constantly changing world. We should not be afraid to try out new technology, new ideas and theories, to change careers and pursue our true interests and goals. There is an innate longing for greatness within all of us. That longing cannot ever be fulfilled without a willingness to change, improve and try something new.

People should not fear starting a second career, even one that begins in mid-life. Naturally, impetuous and ill-thought-out behavior can be disastrous. But in our ever-changing society and economy it is becoming clear that many if not most of us will complete our working career doing something far different than that which we had been trained for when we first entered the workplace. So, wise planning for the future always entails keeping an eye open for new possibilities and situations. The world of the computer, of the Internet and of all its attendant spin-offs, is uncharted territory. But it is the space of the future and we should not allow ourselves to be terrified. One should never be frightened of newfangled equipment. The inquisitive spirit of human beings has invented a world undreamed of by our grandparents. We live in that world, but we also should have an eye out searching for the new world that constantly lurks beyond our field of vision. Progress – physical, political and spiritual – is always contingent upon the willingness to try something new.

Learn to Laugh

We are all able to laugh at good jokes and clever comedies. But these are artificial stimuli to our funnybones. The ability to laugh at life's foibles in a continual and sincere fashion is a necessary quality for pleasant survival and safe sailing in our daily sea of struggles. Healthy laughter must therefore emanate from within the person and not depend on outside forces and situations. Such laughter is a result of the innate ludicrousness of the human condition and behavior. Our Matriarch Sarah, when being informed that she would bear a child after so many decades of barrenness, laughs. Her son is named Isaac (which means "will laugh") in order to immortalize her laughter. Abraham also laughed when G-d informed him of the impending blessing which He intended to bestow upon both of them. Jewish tradition teaches us that Abraham's laughter was one of joy.

Sarah's laughter was one of doubtful wonder. Abraham is rewarded for his laughter. Sarah is criticized because of her laughter. There is apparently laughter and laughter. Laughter of disbelief, bordering on cynicism, is unacceptable. Laughter of joy at the wonders of G-d's world, its surprises and constant unpredictability, is admired and necessary. An obvious lack of laughter at any time is apparently an improper reaction to life's events.

But laughter, in order to be truly productive, has to be inwardly directed. Again, the examples of Abraham and Sarah inform. They laughed inwardly, within themselves, about their own personal situations in life. One has to be able to laugh at one's own mistakes, attitudes and actions. Laughter can be a cruel weapon when it is turned against others. Then it becomes ridicule, something negative that hurts both the laugher and the one who is being laughed at. All great comedians make themselves the butt of their jokes. Allowing one to laugh at oneself is a sign of ultimate self-worth and self-confidence. Practicing laughing at oneself is the ultimate confidence-building exercise. And there is certainly something humorous that happens to each and every one of us every day of our lives. And even if an event does not appear to be funny while it is occurring (such as a meeting with your boss) in retrospect it may be converted into a wry and humorous event (unless of course you have just been fired!). Writers detailing the inanities of everyday modern corporate and business life have made fortunes. Everyone instantly recognizes themselves, their cohorts and superiors, as well as their workday environment, in these books of humor and social satire. The world is an awfully funny place. Recognizing this truth and responding to it with constant inner laughter will make life more bearable and pleasant.

Of course there are situations in life that do not lend themselves to any form of easy laughter. Serious illness, family breakups, and prolonged unemployment and poverty are never things that can simply be laughed away. Yet, even in these areas of human suffering, laughter and a cheerful disposition remain powerful antidotes to the overwhelming depression that the situation can engender. Countless studies have shown that an optimistic demeanor, which is after all a product of internal laughter, is one of the most powerful and effective weapons against many of life's blows. Proverbs teaches us regarding the great woman of valor that "she laughed even unto her final day." Everyone should attempt to have a great and good internal belly laugh every day.

Don't Count Your Chickens

The well-known advice not to count one's chickens before they hatch is a universally held wisdom. However, this little gem of an article advises you not to count your chickens even after they have hatched. Don't count your chickens, period! Now, I know that this can wreak havoc with an accountant's view of an ordered world, but there is wisdom in not counting one's chickens continually and exactly. There is an old Talmudic tradition that blessings fall upon items that are hidden from the eye. This means that there are many things in life better left alone to ripen and develop by themselves, unhindered by human observation and unlimited by human count. Under such benign neglect, things can apparently grow and increase in accordance with G-d's special blessing for them and not be subject to the interference of human influence – of being counted and measured. One of the great and most mysterious discoveries of modern mechanical physics is the rule that one automatically and helplessly alters particles in some way by merely observing or measuring them. This seems to be a physical manifestation of the above mentioned advice of not counting one's chickens, for fear of interfering with any potential increase or blessing that could descend upon them.

But let me leave the spooky world of physics and metaphysics and discuss more elementary and practical areas of life. I know people who are able to purchase an investment with an eye for the long haul and not concern themselves about it for years on end. They do not look up the financial pages daily to see how their investment is faring, nor do they hound their investment counselor incessantly about this investment. I also know people who bleed daily from the gyrations of the investment markets and who follow their investments relentlessly and fanatically minute by minute. I think that these two diametrically opposite policies represent the true priorities of each of the persons involved. Sometimes letting things be is a great talent. Constant control and micromanagement are not very healthy traits in human policy and family life. One should not count one's chickens on an overly regular basis. There are many things in life that are better left alone.

It is nevertheless true that there are times in life when chickens should and must be counted. Knowing when and how to do this is a measure of the stability and maturity that one brings to life's problems and situations. As in all areas of life, balance and moderation, patience and serenity, are the key factors in making these decisions wisely. A parent who panics at his child's first disappointing report card may be overreacting and thereby making the situation worse. A parent who never reacts to a child's report card, good or bad, inflicts emotional hurt on that child. No one wants to be ignored or forgotten. On the other hand, no one wants to be overly controlled and nitpicked. In a process of trial and error, relying on human experience, memory and plain, good old common sense, one can find the right balance for one's behavior in life. Always remembering that our chickens need not necessarily constantly be counted will help those chickens to mature and flourish – and ultimately to let them blessedly hatch.

Bridging the Generations

People want to know who they are. In order to achieve this happy state of self-identity and self-worth, one must have a healthy sense of family and of past. People are like a painting. If they are not placed in a proper frame then their full beauty and potential cannot be appreciated. The proper frame for people is their family and their family's history. We are not born into a vacuum. By not knowing who we are, we cripple our future generations and ourselves. Therefore, there is a real obligation upon the older generation to tell their life's story to the coming generation. By failing to do so, they are robbing their grandchildren of a treasured heritage that is otherwise irreplaceable.

Many times, grandparents do not live in close physical proximity to their grandchildren. It may be that the grandchildren are far too young to understand or appreciate the oral history that the grandparent wishes to impart to them. In such instances – perhaps even in all instances – the grandparent should write a long letter to the grandchildren detailing the many events and incidents which occurred to them during their lifetime. Today, with the magic of video recorders, this can be done in an oral interview where the grandparent just tells the whole story, for hours on end – if necessary – and the record is captured for posterity. Film, like books, has a very long shelf life and therefore this story can be stored for use for many many later generations, even until centuries later. Those of us who are old enough to appreciate our grandparents should insist on interviewing them and making a permanent record, whether in print or on film, of their story. The bridge between generations is the most secure passage known to families. Each side of this bridge, the older generation and their young descendants, should make certain that such a bridge of communication and history is constructed, maintained and preserved.

In Jewish tradition it is incumbent upon the elders of the family to educate their descendants in the laws and lore of the people of Israel. This obligation is central, for instance, to the Seder night of Passover and its ritual and family drama. The young are to ask their questions:

"Why? Who? What? How?" And the elders are to answer and explain and relive over 33 centuries of history with their future generations. In fact, the Seder night and its ritual is the grand generational review and interview in all of Jewish life. Surveys show that even Jews who are not otherwise observant of their religious ritual celebrate the Passover Seder. This is a form of testimony to the power of intergenerational education and curiosity. In our modern society, where the feelings of rootlessness, alienation and impermanence are so rampant and wide-spread, the anchor of family history and generational identity takes on even greater importance and weight. Therefore, the young should ask the old about what was, so that they can have a better sense as to what is. And the older generation should tell the young about the past in order to guarantee that they will not be forgotten and that the hard lessons of their lives will yet serve to help their descendants find their own way to meaningful existence and productive lives.

Don't Argue, Just Debate

We are always amazed when others don't see our point of view and fail to understand the correctness of our position. "How can you be so dense?" is our unspoken – or sometimes unfortunately our outspoken – response to the expressed disagreement with our opinion. It is natural to take the words of disagreement raised against us in a personal manner. And when that happens the temptation to respond in kind is almost irresistible. Thus the discussion deteriorates from a debate into an argument. In my lifetime, I have known many a person who has won a debate. I have never known anyone who has won an argument.

In every home there is ongoing discussion, spoken or silent, between the members of the family. The same never-ending discussion is found in the workplace, in the neighborhood, in fact, in the entire general society of humankind. Since no two human beings are alike in outlook and opinion, differing viewpoints on the same matter will always abound. The Jewish view of the matter, in theory at least, is that "The words of the wise are spoken calmly and softly." Or, in the words of Proverbs, "A soft answer turns away wrath." There is always room for emotion in life. But emotional argumentativeness guarantees that the point one is trying to make will almost certainly be lost in the emotional trauma of the moment. The wise man therefore speaks softly, to the point, and in a fashion that allows the other party to understand his viewpoint and gracefully retreat without the emotional burden of shame, the shame which is always the by-product when argument instead of debate rages.

I have written elsewhere in this book about the horrifying damage that anger inflicts on those who are party or witness to it (see "I Am Mad as..."). When discussion becomes argument, anger invariably arrives on the scene. When discussion is controlled as being debate, there is little room for anger to take over the proceedings. The prophet Isaiah said to Israel: "Let us go forth and debate the matter ..." Debating, even with G-d, is permitted, in fact it is encouraged. Arguing with G-d, cursing in anger and frustration, is forbidden, counter-productive and emotionally and psychologically harmful. Understanding the sometimes subtle difference between debating and arguing is the key to achieving successful interpersonal relationships and family and social peace and harmony.

A final cautionary word must be added to this little essay. There are people, nations, and situations one encounters in life that do not lend themselves to meaningful debate. Debating a Hitler or a Pol Pot would be an exercise in futility. The proper procedure then is not to argue, not to debate, but rather to protect oneself and one's society from the ravages of such maniacal evildoers. Even within a family there may be individuals who are ruinous people and will never be amenable to discussion or debate. The axiom of Theodore Roosevelt, "Speak softly and carry a big stick," is certainly in place in such circumstances and situations. Speaking softly enhances the power and effectiveness of the big stick. Bellicose arguing is oftentimes interpreted as bluff. Debate, when combined with the presence of the big stick, always gains serious and abiding attention.

21

Spend Your Grandchildren's Money

I was once asked – when I was a young man in my 30s and still pretty much a novice in the rabbinate and in life generally – by an older congregant of my synagogue if I could give him some advice regarding a question that was gnawing at his conscience. Since youth, even relative youth, is omniscient I unhesitatingly told him that I would be able to advise him even though I was unaware of what question was nagging at him so persistently. He posed the question to me thusly: "I am 75 years old and still in good health. All my life, I dreamed of taking a trip around the world with my wife, but I had neither the time nor the money to do so while I was working. Now, I find that my wife and I have the time and the money to do so. But, my youngest grandson is about to enter college and has decided that eventually he is going to go to medical school. Rabbi, it takes a lot of money to become a doctor – school, internship, residency, etc. Should I spend my money on my trip around the world with my wife, or should I save the money for my grandson's medical education?"

A person in his 30s rarely can answer such a question posed by a person who is in his 70s. As one becomes older one sees life and its events far differently from the way one saw them decades earlier. Shaw's comment that "youth is wasted on the young" is certainly apt in many of life's situations. Nevertheless, I am satisfied today with the answer that I gave to my questioner 30 years earlier. I told him to go for it, to take the trip, to realize a bit of his life's dream. And he and his wife did so, and eight months later when he returned, he thanked me profusely for my advice. He not only enjoyed the wonders of traveling around the world, but he had absolutely no pangs of conscience about spending his money on himself. He said, "My grandson will make it if he really wants to, even without my help. But I will have no other chance to take a trip around the world." (His grandson, by the way, quit college in his junior year, married a wonderful Orthodox Jewish woman and established a very successful medical supply business, all on his own.)

I remember that when my grandfather died, my mother and my two aunts expected that his three grandchildren would inherit in equal shares the proceeds of his $10,000 insurance policy. They were therefore surprised and perhaps even disappointed when the insurance company reported that my grandfather had borrowed $9,800 on the policy and thus there was not really much money left for us. Later, we found in my grandfather's papers a receipt for the $9,800 from an organization that attempted (and was somewhat successful) to save Jewish families from Hitler's Europe during World War II. I was proud of my grandfather then and I am even prouder now. His grandchildren have made their way in the world without his money, but have inherited his spirit of concern for others. I am happy that my grandfather spent my money!

Count Your Blessings

We all know intellectually that we should be grateful and appreciative for every day of life and health that we have. But emotionally we find it difficult to relate to this simple truth. We may have nine things that go right for us during the course of one day and one thing – albeit a relatively minor one – goes wrong and we become frustrated and depressed. I remember that many times I had a good day at the office but the commuter traffic during the drive home was heavy and taxing. By the time I arrived home to my wife and children the good day at the office was forgotten and the foul mood engendered by the traffic was what I brought home with me. Sensing the destructive nature of such situations on my family life, I began a program of self-conditioning (such as relaxing in the car outside my garage for 10 minutes and allowing the tension within me to dissipate, or listening to some good music on the car radio before entering the house) that eventually allowed me to bring home the good day in the office instead of the bad day of the traffic. I finally began to realize that in every human endeavor there are blessings and negative things. The wise person will count and treasure and then share the blessings, and minimize the effect of the unavoidable negatives of living.

When one is ill or faced with other major problems in life and somehow through the grace of G-d the situation resolves itself or the illness disappears, there is an immediate rush of appreciation for this happy turn of events. In Jewish tradition, a public recitation of a blessing of thanksgiving is mandated. But after a period of time, this feeling of appreciation begins to fade and again one is troubled by the endless frustrations of life. The feeling of thanksgiving and appreciation must therefore be nurtured and reinforced constantly, otherwise we are doomed to lives of sadness and pessimistic bleakness. I remember when I was a child that my beloved grandfather, a saintly Eastern European rabbi far removed from the pace and style of American life, had an operation to remove cataracts from both of his eyes. At that time this procedure was considered major surgery and required a prolonged hospital stay. When my uncle went to the hospital to pick up my grandfather and take him home, I went along for the ride – always a treat for a child in the 1940s. I remember that my grandfather read every billboard that came into view on the drive home, even though none of the billboards had any relevance to him or his lifestyle. But the point was that now he could see! And he appreciated that gift and blessing that all sighted people take for granted.

The rabbis of the Talmud stated that just being alive is the greatest blessing – one which should be treasured and appreciated. Life, family, work, friends, society, are all sources of immense blessings. They are also invariably also sources of friction, disappointment and frustration. Our view of life should not be an image of a never-ending complaint department. Rather, it should be a place of hope and steadfastness. Such an attitude is achieved by counting our blessings consistently and sincerely.

Read and Study History

The immediate reaction of many if not most people to the subject of history is that it is so bo-r-r-r-ing! Generations of social studies professors and exhausted, overworked teachers have contributed immeasurably to this knee-jerk response to the dreaded word "history." But it should be obvious to all that an acute and active sense of history is necessary for success-ful and meaningful living. For an ignorance of history – whether it is family, national or global – produces a lack of perspective on life and its events. It is not that history necessarily repeats itself. It is rather that history allows us to judge current events in a much more intelligent and perceptive fashion.

The truth of this opinion is bolstered by the fact that all dictatorships and totalitarian governments and parties rewrite history to fit their current malicious needs. In this past century, all of the major murderers – Hitler, Stalin, Pol Pot, Mao, etc. – first had to falsify history to their peoples in order to gain power and acceptance. Only by eliminating the truths of history were their deadly but essentially harebrained schemes of social engineering, genocide and conquest able to gain reality and popularity. The absence of historical knowledge allows seemingly normal, even good, people to agree to being unwitting accomplices to heinous crimes simply because they possess no frame of reference for judging their leaders, their current society or themselves. How unfortunate and dangerous it is to live in a vacuum without knowledge of the past. The Bible stresses the necessity for knowledge of history. "Remember the days of the eternal past," it exhorts us. The reasoning behind this is not merely an attempt to help us avoid the pitfall of repeating past mistakes, but to give every generation and individual a frame of reference for the decisions and attitudes that shape our lives and society. Ignorance of history robs us of that necessary frame of reference.

There are many beautifully written and entertaining history books readily available. Any book by Barbara Tuchman, William Manchester, Martin Gilbert, Robert Conquest, Bruce Catton and others of that caliber is certain to capture your attention and interest. The story of man, with all its beauty, heroism, cruelty and folly, is the most fascinating of all stories. No work of fiction can ever equal the drama and sweep of history itself. Children should be introduced to the reading of history at an early age. It should not be a burdensome "social studies assignment" task, such as it is in many schools, but rather a nurturing of the naturally inquisitive and curious nature of children. We all wish to know where we came from and how we got to where we are now. Only history can provide real and abiding answers to those important questions. Not to open the world of history to one's children is an injustice to them and will eventually stunt their intellectual and psychological growth and maturity. It should be emphasized that history is not the study of dates, battles and places, though those things do figure into the study of history. But dates, places and battles can be deadeningly boring. History is rather the fascinating study of people – of real live human beings. They are never boring!

Family Trees

One of the recent cottage industries to flourish in our current society is the production of family trees – pedigrees, if you will. And if you can't come up with the necessary information for a legitimate family tree, there are companies willing and able to construct one for you anyway, through their "research." Preparing family trees is a booming business. I feel that this phenomenon is part of the generally felt craving of our times to find some roots and background stability for ourselves. The modern Western world is to a large extent a world of alienated and rootless people. We all feel like "outsiders" – even those who are perceived by others as being "insiders." We are constantly on the move. According to the latest census statistics the average American moves at least six times in his or her lifetime.

This feeling of never belonging anywhere gives rise to emotional and psychological difficulties. It interferes with our ability to bind with our families and even with our own inner selves. Therefore a family tree, even if not completely accurate or complete, serves as a foundation for ourselves, our sense of being, our self-worth and even our emotional well-being.

In Jewish tradition, the necessity for family trees is built into the framework of the society. *Kohanim*, members of the priestly tribe of Aaron, have special duties, obligations and privileges placed upon them. So too are the *Leviim,* descendants of the Tribe of Levi, also singled out for special rituals and honors in Jewish society. These groups within the Jewish nation have always fiercely guarded their pedigrees and heritage. They even gave themselves special family names to indicate their family tree and line of descent. In general society, people of nobility and/or notoriety (positive or negative!) also fostered in their families the requirement for keeping and updating family trees. A sense of pride of heritage, as well as a genuine fascination with the past, is created in the keeping of a family tree. My father-in-law had 126 great-grandchildren when he died. Our family kept and keeps records of the life events of these children who are now growing into adulthood. This family tree/record-keeping process has bound our family together, scattered geographically as we are, so that there is a feeling of connection and unity within the family. Cousins, especially distant ones, tend to drift apart in life. Family trees are a powerful weapon in arresting that drift.

But what if I know nothing about the past of my family, a situation not uncommon in our world of today. How can I construct any sort of family tree when I am unaware of my grandparents, who they really were and where they came from? Well, then begin your own family tree with yourself and go forward. Many times we cannot resurrect the sadly forgotten past but we can always salvage the here-and-now present. Make this keeping of a family tree a family project. Involve your children and grandchildren in the preparation and maintenance of your family tree. Make it a significant project in their eyes. It will serve as a significant tool in keeping the family together and giving it focus, meaning and direction. And you will love climbing that tree. It will give you the sense of immortality that all of us crave and need. For a tree survives us all.

You Can't Win Them All

There used to be sportsmanship awards for good losers in the major sports' leagues. That is no longer true, for in our time only winners count. The famous statement of Grantland Rice, an American sportswriter of the 1920s – "It makes no difference whether you win or lose, only how you played the game matters" – is worthy only of derisive guffaws in the current world of sports and of life experiences generally in Western society. We are a society of winners, except that we all know from our personal experiences in life that there are many times when we are losers. In fact, everyone at one time or another is to one extent or another, a loser. How to condition oneself to lose once in a while without being overly troubled by that setback is one of the keys to successful living. A baseball player, reflecting on the length of the baseball season in which even the finest team will endure defeat dozens of times, coined the phrase, "You can't win them all." But this phrase applies to all of us and in all of life's situations. We should always attempt to win, but we should be aware that no one wins all the time. Children, at an early age, learn that one doesn't always prevail. But there is a drive within us that allows us to cheat or bully others so that in the short run – this one particular game, for instance – we will be declared the winner. Parents and teachers must impress on children that losing is part of living and that even if we are saddened and depressed over losing, we are not to compound our losing by immoral, anti-social or even criminal behavior in an attempt to win.

There is an art to losing wisely. In business school we are taught that one should always cut one's losses and not throw good money after bad. It takes a strong ego and self-image to realize that we made a mistake, that the investment, house, partnership, job, etc. is just not going to work out for us and that therefore the wisest thing is to extricate oneself as soon as possible from the losing situation. As a lawyer, I was always astounded to see how successful businessmen allowed themselves to become impoverished because they refused to recognize that they also could make a bad mistake. As a school dean, I was equally astounded as to how parents and students would refuse to recognize that some students were not cut out for certain careers and schools. This inability to recognize the reality of temporarily losing in order to win in the long run always had dire consequences for all involved. It is an axiom in our world that being a good loser is a sign of weakness. The truth of the matter is that being a wise and realistic loser – which is really the definition of being a good loser – is an example of great inner strength and fortitude. The strong can deal with losing. The weak have to always win and since that is impossible, they are doomed to constant frustration, tension, anger and self-doubt.

One of my professors in law school taught me that one should have one major defeat early in one's career. "Losing a trial is the best education a young lawyer can ever have" was his lesson. Someone who always wins in his youth will be unable to deal with the eventual defeat that will certainly be sustained later in life. He will be crushed by this defeat since he has never learned the lesson that "You can't win them all." So, in our pursuit of winning, we should always remember that there are times in life when being a good loser is also a triumph.

The Art of Giving

A common misconception people have is that the art of giving is a natural one and either you have a giving nature or you don't. The miser can't help himself from not giving and the generous donor is really only a victim of his own nature and predilections. The thinkers of Judaism differed decisively from this viewpoint. They taught that one could be trained to give, and that one could learn how to be a generous and giving person. And the way to learn the art of giving is simply by giving. One has to train one's hand to be open. Just as a sensible marathon runner cannot awaken one morning and proclaim himself ready to run the grueling race today without first undergoing months of rigorous training and preparation, so too a sensible person realizes that one cannot just get up one morning and say, "Today I'm going to be a giver, a generous person!" Giving takes training.

It must become a habit, and therefore the key to being a giving person is to adopt a daily regimen of giving.

When I was a student in high school, I was discomfited by the passing of the charity box around the synagogue/study hall during the morning prayer services. I found it to be disturbing to my concentration and demeaning to the lofty atmosphere necessary for sincere prayer. With all of the certainty of superior wisdom that a 16-year-old possesses, I complained to the rabbi who was in charge of the prayer services. I also stated that since all of the students really had no money – so that almost everyone put only a penny or two into the charity box – the entire ritual was only an exercise in futility. The wise man patiently explained that if I trained my hand daily to reach into my pocket and give money to charity, albeit only pennies, I would be ready and able to give charity all my life, since my hand would be trained to give. And later in life when I would have more money I would be able to give substantial sums to charity, easily and graciously, because my giving nature had been developed and had become a vital and intrinsic part of me. He apprised me of Maimonides' statement that it is better to give one dollar 50 times than to give $50 one time. It was not the amount of giving that concerned

Maimonides – it was the training of one's hand and nature to give.

There are many forms of training in how to give. Tithing is certainly one of them. A person should have a sense that all of us are only messengers, trustees of our wealth and blessings but not their ultimate owners. This attitude is surely helpful in allowing one to learn how to give. It is far easier to be generous when one realizes that what we give away is ultimately more ours in terms of reward and satisfaction than that which we keep for ourselves. And the habit of giving is not just confined to donating money. A person who is able to give is ready to help others with the personal gifts of time and attention as well. Many times giving away money is far easier than having to give of oneself to others and their needs. Yet we all know that it is this giving of oneself to others that is the most meaningful and productive form of giving. A society of givers is a blessed society.

Learn How to Take

Even though we are cautioned in the Book of Proverbs that "He who despises receiving gifts will live," there are times in life when one must be prepared to receive gifts, honors, and recognition in a graceful and understanding fashion. Those times are mainly when the refusal to do so will cause damage to the sensitivities, well-being and noble ideals of others or of the community at large. One should never refuse a gift from a child, especially one's own child. And that gift, no matter what it is or is not, should never be demeaned or treated lightly in the presence of the child who is the giver. A person who refuses to accept gifts graciously, even from pious motives, is often seen by others as being mean-spirited and self-centered. I know many people who refused to accept communal honors out of a true spirit of humility and selflessness. Nevertheless, such reticent spirit is often detrimental to the very institutions and causes that one is most interested in promoting and aiding.

The law of unintended consequences applies, almost without any exception, to those who have never learned how to take and accept graciously, and in a timely fashion. Their very nobility of motives in refusing to take becomes a source of hurt and divisiveness that easily eclipses whatever moral good their not taking was intended to illustrate.

The above idea is I believe valid for all people and families, but I am convinced that it is vitally necessary and pertinent for all those who hold public positions. I have seen a number of very promising young rabbis who suffered major problems in their communities simply because they were never taught how to accept honors, gifts and appreciation graciously and modestly. There is a fierce streak of independence within all of us. We all want to be able to make it on our own – to be self-sufficient and not dependent upon the generosity of others. And this is a correct and admirable attitude in life. But there are many times when this attitude, positive as it may be, should not be allowed to reign supreme. We must all realize that success in dealing with other human beings and with our communities at large sometimes entails being a taker. The general community applauds givers. It rarely tolerates those who are never takers and who, by this obvious statement of their own independence, thereby unwittingly declare their contempt for the community at large.

Naturally, the habit of taking must be curbed and controlled. It is no honor to be a beggar or a glory seeker. Knowing when to say no to gifts and honors is also an essential talent for successful living. Just as giving requires discernment and judicious behavior so does taking. Acceptance of anything from dubious characters or questionable organizations is foolish and unjustified behavior. Successful living demands balance and moderation in behavior and attitudes. Therefore never taking seems to be as bad a habit as always taking. Since King Solomon was aware that taking is easier than giving, he correctly warned us of the pitfalls of unrestricted taking. One should always be reticent about taking. But one should never be dogmatic about never taking. There is a time and place in all of our lives where and when we should exhibit the good grace of being a wise and noble taker.

Good Neighbor Policy

The great rabbis of the Mishnah extolled the virtue of being a good neighbor. The American poet, Robert Frost, proclaimed that "Good fences make good neighbors." But I don't think that is quite what the rabbis had in mind. Being a good neighbor is a complicated matter, full of contradictions and paradoxes. It means being there and not being there at one and the same time. It implies a sense of community and joint behavior coupled with a strong respect for the other person's privacy and territory. It involves speaking up, suggesting and advising. But it also requires the ability to be silent, to ignore events and words and uncomfortable situations. It involves sharing, borrowing and consulting, but it also involves staying away and not being a burden to the neighbor. Most important, being a good neighbor requires mutual trust, respect and confidence. It is a well-known phenomenon that in our current urban society people can live in the same building and even in adjoining apartments for years on end without having any meaningful contact with one another. This sense of alienation, which is unfortunately a major presence in modern society, is not contributory to being a good neighbor. Nor is it necessarily the definition of a bad neighbor. Rather, it is just being no neighbor.

The essence of being a good neighbor is the ability to communicate to one's neighbor that you are there for him when he needs you. He may never need you or he may regularly need you. That fact alone is really immaterial to one's being a good neighbor. The point that is important above all else is the neighbor's realization that near him is someone who cares about his welfare and can be counted on for help, large or small. This attitude can be communicated between neighbors by simple acts of kindness and consideration. Placing your neighbor's paper on his porch or doorstep, helping him move heavy objects in his backyard, toning down loud music or raucous parties, and sharing good news and joyous occasions are all small but very positive steps in creating good neighborly relationships. We all know that the small things in life count greatly. A friendly greeting, a smiling face, an act of courtesy, all make for being a good neighbor.

The concept of being a good neighbor is in reality the translation of the theory of tolerance into practical everyday life and behavior. All of us are living in a world that contains billions of other people. How we respond to them is the ultimate test of our humanity and goodness. And even though we will never come into contact with all of those other billions of people, we do come into contact regularly and daily with our neighbors at home and at our places of work. It is in these contacts that we are constantly tested and within which we grow and expand. Our personal growth and mental and spiritual maturity are measured by these interpersonal relationships. Being a good neighbor helps one take a giant stride towards being a good person in every sense. It is the training ground for all of the other contests of life that face us daily. In a sense, how one responds to the person next door is the way one responds to all of the other people of the world and to the situations of life which are omnipresent. Perhaps that is why the wise men of the Mishnah placed such a great emphasis on being a good neighbor.

Memory's Power
and Powerful Memories

One of the great gifts of human life is a sense of memory. I do not mean only the ability to cram for a test and remember all sorts of arcane facts, or the power to recall various items of trivia that enable us to be champion board-game players. I refer rather to the long-term memory that creates emotions, loyalties, and attitudes and eventually borders on myth. It is this sense of memory that gives life its flavor and makes each one of us so unique and special. For without such a memory we are truly "vegetables" as far as the world of the spirit and values is concerned, and rootless "vegetables" at that. The memory of the aroma of my mother's kitchen when food was being prepared for the Sabbath or the holidays, the memory of how sparklingly beautiful the Passover Seder table looked to my 4-year-old eyes, the memory of the child's wonder in seeing for the first time a caterpillar metamorphosing into a butterfly – these are the memories that are so vital to meaningful life. And for various reasons, these types of memory are in woefully short supply in today's society, and especially so in much of Jewish society.

The Jewish people as a collective body always prided itself on its acute sense of memory. Israel remembered that the Exodus from Egypt occurred on a Thursday, that the revelation on Sinai took place on the Sabbath, that Rabbi Akiva was executed by the Romans in the hippodrome of Caesarea on Yom Kippur, and that the Jews of Ethiopia are descended from a "peace corps" mission of members of the tribe of Dan whom Solomon sent there at the request of the Queen of Sheba. Such exacting memory also recalled the people who populated the generations of Israel, the great heroes and the despised villains, as well as the historical events surrounding them and the context of the time in which they lived. This sense of memory was based on the obligation of one generation to transmit not only its accumulated knowledge to the next generation, but even more importantly, to transmit to the future generation the very power of memory itself. Jewish parents trained Jewish children to remember – to remember the Land of Israel even though they never saw that land, to remember the covenant with God at Sinai even though adherence to that covenant brought with it sacrifice and difficulties, to remember to be good and kind in a world that lacked compassion – in short, to remember to be a Jew!

Somehow, something happened to us on the way to the modern world. A large section of the Jewish people developed a severe case of amnesia. The transmission of memory from one generation to the next was interrupted. In 19th century Europe and in the Land of Israel there was a studied attempt by the "enlightened ones" – mainly the Left and the self-styled intelligentsia – to destroy all memory of the "old Jew" and replace that person with the "new Jew." The "new Jew" was to be modern and strong and self-reliant. He was also to be atheistic, non-observant of Jewish tradition and lifestyle, and without any sense of long-term memory. His memory span reached back to 1897 or 1948 or 1967 or only to 1994. In the United States, the official Jewish community and many Jewish families consciously and knowingly destroyed Jewish memory, feeling that this destructive act was a necessary prerequisite to becoming fully Americanized. Memory, it was felt, would inhibit assimilation, and for most of this past century the goal of mainstream

American Jewry – its organizations, its movie-makers, its authors, and its leaders and even its clergy – was assimilation. Well, in Israel we now have the "new Jew" who is not so happy with his "newness" and travels to Nepal to find Far Eastern gurus to attempt to cure his amnesia. And the American Jewish community, shrinking in numbers and influence, drowning in a sea of materialism, spiritual malaise and indifference to its ultimate fate, has become the most assimilated of all Jewish communities in history. Such are the rewards of enforced amnesia.

Years ago when my wife and I, and our little children, moved from Chicago to Miami Beach, Florida, to assume our roles as the rabbinical family for a small Orthodox congregation, we felt very lonely. Our families were in Chicago and Detroit and for me it was not only a change of locale but of profession as well. We needed some tender loving care, but usually a rabbi's congregants don't think of themselves as being obligated to fulfill that role. However, the Gellers, a sweet, unassuming, gentle, and deeply religious couple, in their noble way, became surrogate grandparents to our children, who sorely missed their own biological grandparents. Miami Beach is hot and humid for seven to eight months of the year. When we moved there, the homes generally were not completely air-conditioned as they are today. Yet this elderly Mrs. Geller would bake us a fresh loaf of Sabbath bread (*challah*) every Friday even though the temperature in her non-air-conditioned kitchen must have reached sauna level. She did this for us every Friday of the year, and her husband would walk over in the hot afternoon sun to deliver the loaf of delicious Sabbath bread. Our children were raised on Mrs. Geller's *challah*. It was the highlight of our week, our anchor to holy Sabbath memories.

We eventually moved from Miami Beach and later, in the fullness of time, the Gellers also left – they to move on to their eternal reward. Our children married and are now raising children of their own. Somehow they transmitted the memory of Mrs. Geller's *challah* to our grandchildren who had never seen or known her. My wife and I have always celebrated our Sabbath with the memory of Mrs. Geller's *challah* being present with us at the table. Therefore, imagine my joy when I spoke at a public event in Jerusalem before this past Rosh Hashanah, and a woman approached me and said, "I am Mrs. Geller's granddaughter and I have baked a *challah* for your Sabbath table and here it is!" Our memories converged to create an emotional bond that transcended the passage of time and the change of location. The great task of life had been accomplished – memory had been transferred from one generation to the next.

The Jewish people needs a good stiff dose of memory to help it cope with the difficult problems it faces in every part of the world. Each individual person and family should dread the affliction of Jewish amnesia. It is never too early or too late to fight this amnesia and to develop Jewish memory. Our task in life is not only to remember and transmit memory to future generations. We also should recognize our obligation to create the "stuff" from which memories are made. Our success in so doing will be the measure of our stature in the never-ending story of Israel.

Clothes Make the Man

There is perhaps nothing that communicates instantly to others who we are, or who we think we are, as much as the clothing that we wear. In a time and society of casual dress, even in the office and workplace, there is a tendency to ignore the important psychological message that clothing transmits, not only to others, but to the wearer. The truth of the matter is that clothing that we like, that we are proud of, helps build confidence and self-esteem. Sports teams, armies, civil servants, students, religious affiliates and many other groupings in our society all wear uniforms and place great emphasis upon their design and appearance. Napoleon commented, "It is amazing how a man will risk his life for a piece of ribbon." And the truth is that "a piece of ribbon" does lift our spirits and speaks to our inner need for recognition and self-worth.

I am a tie aficionado. Nothing lifts my spirits like a new tie. Ties to me are not just clothing but are my teddy bear and security blanket. Buying new clothing is, on the whole, probably cheaper than going to a psychiatrist on a regular basis. In many faiths, communities and religions, the holy days of the year are marked by the custom of wearing new clothing. Nothing, not even a new shiny toy, excites a child's heart and brings it as much pleasure and pride as new clothing. And we all remain children at heart, no matter what our chronological age. So, don't think of clothing as just a physical necessity, or an unnecessary indulgence. It should be seen as good healthy therapy that aids us in maintaining our identity and self-pride in a sometimes hostile world.

Long ago, four of my friends and I began dating in the hope of finding the "right" one quickly. We were all monetarily poor, certainly by today's standards. None of us had a car and we, neither individually nor collectively, could afford to take a girl to a concert, or to any other event that entailed spending real money for tickets of admission. So we hit upon the brilliant idea that we would pool our meager financial assets and purchase one good, expensive 100-percent silk tie. We were certain that this tie would impress the maiden to such an extent that she would be happy and satisfied merely sharing a glass of soda pop and conversation during the evening. We divided our social calendars in such a way that the tie would be available to each of us when needed. Once, one of my friends came back in a very crestfallen mood from a date with a girl in whom he was especially interested. I asked him what the problem was. He responded that the girl told him, "I already went out with that tie before." Nevertheless, the tie gave us the courage to court our future wives with a sense of confidence. So, never underestimate the ego-building impact of clothing.

I Can't or Can't I?

People have the strange habit of selling themselves short, of betting against themselves. Perhaps it is the fear of failure that prevents us from pushing ourselves to attempt great things. "I can't do it!" is a terrible self-indictment, and the worst part of it is that often I certainly "can do it," but by not risking the attempt to "do it" I crush my own ego and creative drive permanently. To be successful at anything in life – career, marriage, family, social relationships – requires investment in self. The defense mechanism of self-denigration cripples us and prevents us from taking advantage of the opportunities that life constantly presents. A person must always strive for improvement, for a higher view and a deeper commitment, for the right way for oneself, and not for the easy and non-challenging path.

It is not enough to vaguely believe in a cause or goal.

One must be willing to sacrifice and risk much to justify that belief. I once taught a student who was convinced that he would never gain admittance to medical school because of his average math grades. Even though he had a high overall grade average, in fact a truly superior grade average if the math scores were factored out, he refused to send applications for admission to medical schools and he did not attempt to sit for the M-Cats exam. When he came to commiserate with me, I pointedly said to him, "You really don't want to become a doctor. You are using your math scores as an excuse not to pursue a medical career. If you really wanted to be a doctor, you would invest the time and sacrifice necessary to be accepted into medical school. You purposely sell yourself short in order to avoid the rigors of medical school and of the medical profession itself. If you decide that you really wish to be a doctor, you will become a doctor!"

The student's mother called me later in the day to reprimand me for speaking so strongly to her son. She said, "If he can't do it, he can't do it. There is no necessity to make him feel guilty about it." But I believed that he could do it and that, with her tacit encouragement, he was selling himself very short, and I told her so. The happy ending to the story is that today the young man is an excellent surgeon, and his mother is proud and delighted with his success. She is still angry with me for making her son feel guilty, but I am more aware than ever before of the tragic error of selling oneself short.

Yet, are there not things, goals, challenges, that are beyond us? Are there not occasions when "I can't do it" is really the proper response? The answer to that is definitely "Yes." If someone would ask me to perform emergency brain surgery or swim the English Channel, I certainly would answer, "I can't do it." But that is a realistic response to a particular situation, not an attitude towards life generally. If there are too many situations in life that elicit from us the response "I can't do it," then this becomes a problem of attitude and viewpoint. Perhaps not everyone can climb to the top of the mountain, but certainly no one should willingly choose to remain at the bottom of the hill because of the fear of not reaching the top. In sports, forfeiting a game counts as a loss. In life, forfeiting an attempt to rise to new heights is also a loss.

32

Ask for Directions

One of the more inexplicable propensities of males (females generally are not guilty of this pattern of behavior) is to avoid having to ask someone for directions. I have gone miles out of my way when driving my car rather than stop at the gas station and ask for directions. It is my unfailing belief in my innate excellent sense of direction, coupled with my ego which always tells me that I really do know how to get to my destination, that causes my stubbornness to dominate me. And so I wander around roads and streets, with my teeth solidly clenched, knowing that I am close to my destination but not really quite there yet. Of course, all the while I refuse to stop and ask for directions, because somehow I sense that so doing would be an admission of failure on my part. For that reason, car makers have installed a very optional feature consisting of an on-board computer screen that is connected to a space satellite that will give one – and show one on the screen – the exact directions needed to arrive at one's destination. Ninety-eight percent of the time one will not really need this gadget, because one could just stop and ask for directions. But since we seem to abhor doing so, this expensive car option has a wonderfully successful future ahead of it.

Asking for directions in other aspects of life is also in order. One of the sad traits of our society is its reluctance to take advice or take direction from anyone. We constantly seek advice from "experts" but we rarely heed that advice. It is a very lonely world if one is forced to make all of the decisions of life alone, unaided and unguided. One should have friends, family, mentors, counselors, to whom one can turn for advice and direction. It is a sign of wisdom and strength to ask others whom we respect and admire for their opinions and guidance. This is true as far as every facet of daily life is concerned – health, career, investment, education, etc. It is certainly true as far as spiritual and emotional concerns are involved. In fact, it is downright foolish to attempt to constantly go it alone in life, without bothering to ask for direction. Jewish tradition has always emphasized the necessity for role models and direction-givers. "Create for yourself a teacher/spiritual mentor/rabbi," was the maxim of the wise men of Israel. Never travel miles in life needlessly, when the right directions, given by others, sometimes even perfect strangers, could spare you that travail.

Asking for direction can often be a humbling experience. But it need not be so. It is basically a learning experience, a growing experience, an opportunity to benefit from humankind's collective memory and experience. Whenever I feel that I have gained in knowledge and outlook from others, I feel newly proud and not embarrassed by my previous ignorance and error. I have goals to achieve, just as you do. Anyone who can help me reach those goals and guide me to them easily and more painlessly, is to be treasured by me. It is the truly wise and sensible person who is clever enough to stop and ask for directions on life's roads. Never pass the gas station that can refuel your spirit, energy and wisdom.

33

Letting Bygones be Bygone

An American maxim, attributed to a legendary football coach, is: "Don't get mad; get even." Perhaps that philosophy of life makes sense in the brutal world of professional football, but it is a disastrous prescription for life in general. For "getting even" certainly inflicts as much harm on the one taking revenge as on the victim of that revenge. Revenge is an all-consuming emotion that can easily become the focal point of one's life, forcing one to always concentrate on negative values and filling one with hatred and bitterness. Revenge rarely corrects past wrongs. It does not afford emotional relief to the avenger, for no act of revenge can ever compensate, in the eyes of that avenger, for the original wrongdoing. Thus no emotional closure is ever achieved, and the residue of negative bitter feelings remains long after the "getting even" part is over.

Forgiveness, or perhaps even better put, acceptance of the past, is a much more emotionally mature and healthy response to the problems of life, especially as it relates to the "problem people" who somehow become part of our lives. This type of forgiveness allows us to put the past behind us, since we cannot in any way change what has already occurred. If someone has caused you great pain and obviously doesn't realize it, or worse, doesn't care about it, then the healthy reaction is to "forget" about that person. Don't have contact with him or her, don't let that person dominate your thoughts and life. Good, simplistic advice, you will say, but what about family situations? What if the person who has hurt you and harmed you is your sibling, or in-law, or even your child? The emotional pain then is so strong that it becomes almost impossible to let go, to ignore, to accept, let alone to forgive. But again, even then, revenge is not an answer. The attempt to remove that person from your life – emotionally, socially and mentally – is the key to your own well-being. Never let your life be dominated completely by the actions and negative attitudes of others, no matter how close those others are or were to you. It is not easy to accomplish such closure, but it is a much wiser path in life than being overcome by the desire for revenge or for punishment of others.

All of this having been written, one should realize that society as a whole must punish lawbreakers and take action against criminals and terrorists. "Having mercy on the brutal criminals eventually leads to being cruel towards the merciful" is a maxim of the Talmud. We must differentiate between societal revenge and the fallacy of personal revenge. Society must have rules and those rules must be enforced. Yet, even in cases of societal rules for revenge, society makes provision for forgiveness. Pardons and amnesties are also part of the social fabric. Obsessing about past crimes denies emotional closure to societies, not only to individuals. The belief in a just G-d, though His rewards and punishments are never really discernible by mortal humans, is a great aid in achieving an attitude of acceptance and forgiveness on a personal level. "Vengeance is the L-rd's" remains a truism throughout all generations. To humans is left the task of acceptance and eventual forgiveness.

Singin' in the Rain

Taking an unnecessary walk in the rain was always thought of as evidence that one was in love or slightly daft (sometimes these two states of being coincide). Aside from the discomfort of becoming thoroughly wet and the accompanying danger of catching a nasty cold, walking in the rain is seen as being a purposeless exercise. Yet, there is something within us that responds favorably to walking in the rain. The song, "Singin' in the Rain," was wildly popular in its day, a time of financial, military and global turmoil. Even in times of discomfort and trial, people sing. Perhaps even more so in such times than in better days. Because we are all optimists by nature and share a collective feeling that the world can and will be made better, we sing even in the rain. For eventually the rain ends, and in retrospect we see the rain as having been a blessing, in spite of the temporary discomfort and annoyance it may have caused us.

In this respect, rain symbolizes many other occurrences which are beneficial in the larger picture of life, though they are troublesome and uncomfortable at the time they occur. The wise person "sings" whenever and however it rains. Life is by its very nature unpredictable. As much as we attempt to order and secure our lives, we are eventually forced to confront the unexpected, the surprising, even the most dismaying happenings in life. "Into each life some rain must fall" is a well-known maxim. Being able to sing in that rain is a most important trait for successful living. And in order to sing, one must have a very long-range, optimistic view of one's life. The rabbis of the Talmud had their own maxim for viewing life's events: "Everything that our All-Merciful Father does is for the good." We all know stories of planes and trains missed, positions and jobs lost, even of sad and tragic happenings that somehow in the end turned out to be favorable events and not the disasters they originally appeared to be. It is the very uncertainty of life that guarantees a suspension of judgment regarding current events. One can only take them in stride, do one's best, hope and pray for the best, and retain a positive attitude towards life and its events.

I have always maintained that history has the final vote in human events. By that I mean that all certainties of life are subject to the final editing process of history and events. One can never be certain while it is raining whether to sing or weep. Only much later, again in retrospect and in the perfect vision of hindsight, do our choices and answers appear in clarity. Because of this, I always have felt that the sagest course in life is to sing in the rain. It certainly allows one to deal with life's problems in a coherent and upbeat manner, even when one is caught in the rain without an umbrella.

Ruled by the Clock

have a friend who is a stickler for being on time. In fact, I would say that much of his life revolves about being on time for meetings, gatherings, meals, entertainment events and just about everything else. He once told me, only half-facetiously, that he preferred attending funerals rather than weddings, because funerals always start on time. Now, I am a firm believer in using time wisely, being on time for appointments, and keeping time accurately. After all, time is probably the only thing in life that is irreplaceable and cannot ever be retrieved. But being a slave to time, to rigid punctuality, to the unbending demands of the clock, has profound and sometimes even tragic drawbacks.

I lived in the New York City area for over 25 years, and because of the impossible traffic conditions that prevail there, I often found myself running late for appointments and speaking engagements. This happened to me frequently, even when I purposely left my suburban home early with seemingly plenty of time to spare. In fact, in my zeal for punctuality, I once arrived at a wedding – where I was to be the officiating clergyman – before the bride, groom, caterer and florist showed up! Eventually, after a few years, I learned to take my encounters with time in stride. I reckoned that my speaking engagements wouldn't start without me, and I developed a few good apologetic anecdotes to use in those cases where I was late. I never became callous about time, but I resolved never to be imprisoned by the unyielding challenge posed by the hands of the watch-face.

Being punctual is a great character trait. However, it should not be the overriding concern of one's being. Many a motor car accident is traceable to punctuality taking precedence over safety, prudence and common sense. We become annoyed and angry at our own beloved ones (especially spouses!) because of tardiness of a few minutes. This often leads to more serious arguments and increased interpersonal tensions. The few minutes of time lost when someone is late are clearly not worth the terrible fallout of such confrontations. I know people who purposely set their clocks ahead or behind 10 or 15 minutes in order to escape the tyranny of being "on time." I have never quite figured out how this action solves the problem, but it certainly illustrates how time dominates us, to the extent that we have to fool it or fool ourselves. Time is relative, not just in physics, but in everyday normal human existence. As such, it should be assigned an important place in our lives, but certainly not the most important place.

Take the Long Way

All of us love to find shortcuts. Often the shortcut proves to be the really long way, fraught with perils, disappointments and dangers that we never imagined existed. Most evil behavior and criminal acts are in reality only shortcuts to what may be legitimate goals, but the long way usually involves a seemingly greater investment of time and effort than that demanded by the shortcut. Thus, the shortcut always looks more appealing to us. But, if there is no free lunch in life, so too, life provides no real shortcuts. The long way home is the sure way home. We are impatient by nature, disturbed by petty details, tyrannized by watches and clocks, and we therefore easily fall prey to the shortcut syndrome. Don't do it! The "easy buck," the "quick deal," and the "cutting of corners" have ruined many a potentially good person and wreaked havoc on an otherwise stable family group.

Recently, I saw what, to my mind, was a perfect illustration of the dangers of the "shortcut" syndrome. I was on a tour bus which was transporting some 50 people from the airport to a hotel. There was heavy traffic on the road and the bus was making slow progress. We came upon a brand new highway with signs indicating that this highway would lead us to the center of the city where the hotel was located. It appeared to be the ideal shortcut. However, since no vehicles were using this new highway, we passengers were suspicious of its worth. The bus driver, however, insisted that he was not going to waste any more of his valuable time creeping along the road in heavy traffic when this inviting shortcut was so clearly available. So we went roaring along this new, empty, traffic-free highway for about two miles, until suddenly the bus driver desperately applied the brakes and brought the bus to a squealing stop. We were only a few feet away from the bank of a sizable chasm – with a river running at its base – that had as yet not been bridged. The bus driver had to back up the bus miles to the original road and we resumed our tedious but much more certain journey to the hotel. Shortcuts are often very deceiving. They can even be fatal.

There are other advantages in taking the long way. For quite a number of years, I lived in a suburb of a very large city and I commuted to my work by automobile. (My work then required that I have a car at my disposal at all times during the day.) Traffic was always a terrible hassle and I found myself coming home every night in a foul, tense, grouchy mood (see "Count your Blessings"). This severely impacted on the general atmosphere at our supper table, and my relationship with my wife and children began to suffer. So I hit upon the idea of taking the long way home, of driving around the beautiful park in our suburban village, of letting all of my tension drain from me before actually arriving at the driveway to my home. Taking the long way home worked a transformation within me and certainly improved the atmosphere at home and my relations with my family. Sometimes, I would even sit in the automobile for a period of time after I was already parked in my driveway, because I felt that I was still too tense. Better to enter the home later in a decent frame of mind than earlier in a bad temper, I reasoned. When my children would ask me, "Daddy, why are you later than usual tonight?" I would always answer, "I took the long way home."

Can You Keep a Secret?

Can you keep a secret? Unfortunately, many of us cannot. The basis of all professionalism in such careers as the clergy, medicine, law, accounting and financial planning is the sacred presence of confidentiality and privacy. Professionals in these fields who cannot keep a secret are doomed to failure, if not worse, in their careers. Yet, in spite of this ethical standard, the tendency to be loose-lipped about the facts entrusted to us by others is at an epidemic proportion in our society. There are always informed "leaks" from all secret meetings and negotiations, both in regard to government and to private enterprise. There is no right to privacy for any successful or noteworthy person. The press and the other members of the media have erected a new golden calf called "the right to know." Gossip columns flourish, while lurid, and in the main grossly exaggerated if not downright false, stories about public and private people fill the magazines and TV channels. People who reveal secrets about others are rewarded and those who do keep secrets are seen as naive, if not downright subversive. But, my friends, there is a great triumph of self in keeping a secret.

In my life experience as a lawyer, businessman, public administrator, and as a rabbi, I know a great many secrets about a great many people and events. I even imagine that I could write an interesting "tell-all" book about my various careers in life, and about the people I have encountered along the way. But this would in no way compare to the sheer joy and feeling of accomplishment that I have had over the years as I kept these secrets confidential. I was loyal to my trust and to the feelings of confidence that people placed in me. As such, I am rewarded to a far greater extent than any monetary or noteworthy honor could afford me. To realize that people trusted in me, and that I kept their trust, lowers my blood pressure by 20 points. It is the satisfaction gained by knowing that people are truly helped by my silence, by my inaction, by my keeping my mouth closed, (which is no easy task) that provides me with the warmth and glow of doing what I innately know is right.

All rules have exceptions. There are times when the safety of society and individuals requires that secrets be revealed. Many a good literary and cinema plot has revolved about a clergyman or lawyer or doctor knowing a terrible secret that has been confided in him and being confronted by the moral dilemma of whether, when and how to reveal it to the authorities or to others. But most of us are not privy to those types of secrets. We deal with small secrets of others' hopes and opinions, plans and aspirations. It is a weakness within us that allows us to blurt out what those others have told us in confidence and trust. If you want to start feeling good about yourself, then develop the knack and habit of keeping a secret. Not revealing the first secret within you is the hardest test. After a while, keeping secrets will become second nature. You will then be amazed at what this simple accomplishment of keeping a secret will do for your self-esteem and psychological health, not to speak of your moral standing with others.

Listening Is More
Than Just Hearing

There was a terrific sign that I once saw hanging in an office. It proclaimed: "Do not engage mouth unless you are certain that brain is in gear." Speech, which is G-d's great gift to man and which differentiates humans from all other creatures, is often abused, since it is so taken for granted. The ability to talk is so natural to us that we give it little thought and short shrift. Therefore, all of us say a lot of stupid things. We have a tendency to engage in one-sided conversations – intent upon delivering our message – and therefore we are not really able to listen to what the other person is telling us. Successful people train themselves in the art of becoming good listeners. Listening is more than just hearing. It affords one the ability to discern the real intent of his fellow-conversationalist and to judge carefully what the correct response to his words should be. Therefore, the key to being a good conversationalist, to being able to talk with wisdom and tact, is to be a good listener. We teach our children to talk, but rarely do we invest any effort in teaching them to listen. Learning to listen is a fantastic skill.

I remember that at the beginning of my law career, I attended a negotiating conference regarding the possibility of settling a lawsuit for a considerable amount of money. My main tasks at that meeting were to guard the briefcase of the senior partner of our law firm, to look wise, and to keep my mouth absolutely shut. As the negotiations wore on, with apparently both sides speaking at each other and not to each other, very little progress was being made. I was fascinated by the skill of the rhetoric of the negotiators, but I was perplexed by the fact that neither side was really listening to the proposals advanced by the other side. Each side was fixated on its own negotiating position and insisted on its adoption as being the final method of settling the dispute. Suddenly, my senior partner – apparently sensing that even a smaller settlement than originally demanded would be more advantageous to our client than actually going to full trial – changed his approach. He made a key concession that seemingly opened the way for a final settlement to be reached. The opposing lawyer ignored the new offer being made and continued only to parrot his original position. He did not even hear, let alone listen to, the new offer being advanced. The negotiating session ended without agreement, the case went to trial, our side somehow won (juries are fickle bodies of people) and the advantages that the opposing lawyer could have secured for his now hapless client disappeared. All because he was more interested in talking than in listening.

Cultivating a good ear to be able to hear others is an art and a skill. Physicians, psychologists, lawyers and other professional counselors are trained to distinguish between listening and merely hearing. Don't finish other people's sentences for them. Don't formulate your answer until you have heard the complete question being asked. Don't prejudge a conversation. Listen carefully to what your children say to you. The conversation may not be important to you but it certainly is to the one speaking to you. If you should look before you leap, you certainly should listen before you speak.

Don't Be a Nay-sayer

One of the most deadly words in any language is the one that represents the idea of "No!" There are those who have made a habit of responding "No!" to almost everyone and everything. The nay-sayers of the world, if not constituting a majority of humans, certainly are numerous and ubiquitous among us. We encounter them whenever we come up with a new idea, a different plan, a bold and adventurous scheme. The nay-sayers never volunteer to work on community projects; they never compliment the good-doers; they never encourage the young to try something different and new – they only say "No! It will never work." Such has been the reaction of the nay-sayers to every technological advance and invention since the discovery of the wheel and the plow. The amazing thing is that the true nay-sayer, while now acknowledging the worth of the latest invention which he was so quick to dismiss as being impossible, remains the very same, stubborn nay-sayer when another new and as yet untried invention is proposed and explored. The nay-sayer never admits that everything is possible. He revels in the belief that all imagined things and new ideas are really impossible and not worthy of investment and further pursuit.

The nay-sayer is indigenous to all communal committees, boards of trustees/governors, bureaucratic departments, school administrations and bank boardrooms. "That is not the way we do things around here" is the self-righteous motto of the nay-sayer. Such an attitude stifles creativity, discourages the young who are everhopeful for improvement and change, and stigmatizes the truly gifted as being "crazy." Every major innovation and invention in ancient and modern times had its opponents and detractors who decried it even before it was ever tried and put to the practical test of use. This is true not only in terms of physical tools and inventions, but as far as intellectual and spiritual creativity is concerned as well. Every new commentary to the Talmud, every new translation of ancient texts into modern vernacular language, every attempt to introduce new and fresh methodology into the teaching of youngsters – all encounter the nay-sayers at the gates. "Not necessary," "Too different," "Out of line with what has gone before," are some of the stock phrases of the wisdom of the nay-sayers. But the truth is that they are the ones who are wrong. Saying "No!" certainly has a place in our daily lives and encounters. However, saying "No!" continually and regularly to everything in life renders one a negative and pessimistic person. Nay-sayers are depressing people.

Children go through a stage called "the terrible twos." They are not pleasant to be around during this stage of their behavior development, and even grandparents are hard-pressed to love their offspring when they are in the throes of "the terrible twos." Most people eventually outgrow "the terrible twos." But not all people. The nay-sayers in life are 40- and 50-year-old "terrible twoers." Never see yourself as a nay-sayer. More importantly, never allow others to see you as being a nay-sayer.

Small Stuff Adds Up

There is an interesting book on the market entitled, "Don't Sweat the Small Stuff – and It's All Small Stuff," by Dr. Richard Carlson. This book has sold millions of copies in the United States and is full of uplifting and healthy attitudes toward life, its problems and its woes. None of my books has (as of yet) sold millions of copies, so I continue with this short essay in all proper humility. The truth of the matter is that the small things matter mightily in life. The author is right in saying that life, for most of us, is "all small stuff." My opinion, however, is that one *must* "sweat the small stuff." It is the only way to complete the puzzle of our lives in a satisfactory and productive manner.

It is the "small stuff" that colors our lives, that frustrates or illuminates our existence. Children remember the "small stuff" of their childhood; students always recall the "small stuff" of their school years; and the success or failure of both marriages and businesses is usually dependent on "small stuff." To consider the "small stuff" of life as truly being small stuff is very dangerous.

Now, I am well aware that the author of the "Small Stuff" book means that we should not be undone by the petty and relatively unimportant things in life, and he is certainly correct in advising that we should not allow the "small stuff" to unnerve us. However, I am equally certain that we have to be very careful in how our "small stuff," affects others. King Solomon, in Proverbs, stated the matter in his usual direct way: "Dead flies make even the most perfumed oils repugnant." One dead fly, the proverbial "fly in the ointment," is sufficient to undo a lifetime of effort and accomplishment. A dead fly is really only "small stuff" compared to perfumed oils. Yet history is replete with small instances and seemingly minor occurrences that altered the shape of mankind. A foolish law, an unguarded remark, or an insult, even if unintended, can and has sparked revolution, turmoil and destruction. Life is all "small stuff," but in adding it all together the "small stuff" becomes really "big stuff."

Central to the idea of spirituality and serenity in life is the idea that, as far as I am concerned, there really is no "small stuff." What we do and say, why we laugh and cry, how we interact with others, is all somehow important to our souls and psyches. Concentrating on our own "small stuff," while at the same time ignoring the "small stuff" that life and others throw at us, insures us a better chance for mental health and spiritual inner peace. Try and watch your "small stuff" for one day and you will be amazed at the difference it makes not only in your day, but in your life.

It Really Can Be a Good Morning

It is quite understandable that not everyone always feels cheerful upon arising in the morning. The anticipation of the workday and its possible frustrations can have a definite effect on one's mood. Yet, for others as well as for oneself, there can be no greater downer in life than beginning the day by giving or being the recipient of a sour look or, perhaps worse yet, by being pointedly ignored by another human being. Moral wisdom I received as well as my own personal experience has taught me that the best way to prevent this scenario from taking place is to greet other people with a polite, friendly (but not insanely cheerful), "Good Morning." At no time of the day is the Talmudic adage, "Greet each person with a pleasant demeanor," more applicable than in the morning. Most people, after recovering from the shock your greeting will have inflicted upon them, will respond in kind, and both you and the other person will then be on the way to a more pleasant day.

Emotions and moods are often direct results of specific behavior. Thus, polite behavior, good neighborliness and demonstrable human concern can create a more serene mood, lower blood pressure, and enable one to overlook pesky but petty annoyances. A positive consequence of all this is that one can then proceed with the task at hand in a better frame of mind. And to think that all of this can flow from just one "Good Morning" said to a total stranger! As with all human kindness, this action becomes a spiritual, G-dly act, and should never be dismissed as mere manners. While it may be possible to be polite and yet not overtly religious, I think it is impossible to grow spiritually without demonstrating consideration and politeness to other human beings.

A number of years ago, during my then regular summer vacation visit to Jerusalem, as I was going to the morning prayer service at the neighborhood synagogue, I met a man walking his dog. I said, "Good morning," (in flawless Hebrew) to him, but he completely ignored me and kept on walking. This scenario repeated itself every morning for an entire month, I saying "Good morning" and he never responding. When I returned to Jerusalem the next summer, I again met him and his dog on the same morning route. Not having learned my lesson, I again said, "Good morning." There was no response, but I persevered, and after about a week the dog began to recognize me and barked at me as I said "Good morning" to its master. I felt that progress was being made and even though my human friend had not cracked as of yet, I continued my "Good morning" for the balance of my stay. However, on my third summer visit, not only did the dog bark, but its owner finally grunted in response. Finally, over the weeks, we even began to have small conversations and somehow, by the time I left at the end of that summer, I felt that we were friends. When I returned to Jerusalem the following summer, I met my friend on his morning route but he was without the dog. He sadly informed me that his dog had died and that he was now walking alone every morning. He said, "That dog taught me a great lesson in life. Now, I say 'Good morning' to the garbage men, the street cleaner, anyone I meet in the morning. It makes the day easier for me. I am not so alone, and I am still able to feel that I am walking my faithful dog."

I Am Mad as ...

Anger is the most destructive character fault that humans possess. It leads to hatred, violence, inner turmoil and depressing unhappiness. Anger is the most common form of insanity, so common, unfortunately, that it is not recognized generally for its nihilistic qualities. For when a person acts or speaks in anger he has lost control of himself, and that loss of control will always have deleterious if not even tragic consequences. In an unconscious but unerringly true slip of the tongue, when we are angry we say, "I am mad as...," and when we allow our anger to control us and our behavior, we are at that moment truly mad. Slow to anger and easily calmed when angry, are traits to be pursued and practiced. G-d Himself, so to speak, describes His attributes in these terms. We are bidden to imitate our Creator, and slow to anger is a good place to begin.

The great Maimonides, always the champion of moderation and of the golden mean in human behavior, allows for only two extremes – extreme humility and lack of anger. Anger destroys families, careers, noble enterprises, and even nations, and it can topple world order and stability. Anger begets abuse, both emotional and physical. It demeans our own internal self-judgment and undermines our feelings of self-worth, eventually turning our wrath inward upon ourselves. Woe to any situation where the matter which is to be settled, or even discussed, is dealt with in anger. As our sages say concerning every person who becomes angry, "If he is a sage, his wisdom departs from him; if he is a prophet, his prophecy departs from him."

Well, then, how do we control and diffuse our anger? Though there are no magic answers to this question, I am bold enough to tell you of my own experience. As I am somewhat of a public figure, there have been situations in which I have felt anger. On one such occasion when I shared my feelings of anger (about an issue which I later realized was of petty concern) with my father-in-law, who was older and wiser than I, he told me the following anecdote. When he was an adolescent attending school, he boarded at the home of a great and sainted rabbi/teacher. One day, he noticed that the rabbi became angry while speaking with a family member. Immediately excusing himself from the conversation, the rabbi went to a corner of the room and conducted a monologue, explaining to himself the futility and corrosive nature of anger, until finally his feelings of anger were dissipated. He then resumed his previous conversation in a calm and measured manner.

Similarly, Abraham Lincoln wrote angry rejoinders to the editors of newspapers that had reviled him. However, he never sent those letters, preferring instead to keep them in his desk while his anger cooled. Just the act of composing those letters provided the necessary catharsis. We all know that anger is bad for us. We only need "someone" to periodically remind us of that fact. Sometimes the best "someone" for this task is one's own self. Anger is the insanity. Talking to oneself in order to diffuse that anger is not.

Don't Argue With the Referee

One of the cardinal rules in all sports and games, one which is honored more in its breach than in its observance, is the advice of the coach/manager: "Don't argue with the referee/umpire. He never changes his call. You will only antagonize him, and furthermore you will probably sulk even more intensely as you simmer over the unfairness of a bad decision. You consequently lose the concentration necessary to enable you to play at your best." This is all true, and so is the fact that excessive arguing usually brings with it greater retaliatory punishments such as fines, ejection from the game, or even suspension from future games.

Yet, we all know that all players and even all coaches/managers do sometimes argue with the referee. It is human nature to protest against what we perceive as injustice, unfairness or excessive cost. We all rail against an unreasoning fate and its harshness and inconvenience. We waste a great deal of our energy and spirit on the question of "Why?" which ultimately has no answer in this world. A number of years ago, the National Football League instituted a system for second-guessing its referees, called "instant replay." The "instant replay" system proved a failure and was eventually discontinued. One of the reasons for this failure was that cameras operating from different angles on the field "saw" things differently, so that the matter was no clearer after the viewing of the "instant replay" film than it was on the basis of the decision of the referee alone. It all depended on the camera's angle and location.

The ultimate Referee of life is our Creator, Who does not easily change decisions, nor explain them. It is therefore counter-productive to our best interests to allow ourselves to be consumed with arguing with the Referee. Life involves acceptance, playing the hand that is dealt us, doing our best, overcoming adversity and setbacks, hoping and, above all, doing and serving. Raging against the sea of what is *bashert* (preordained) or daring to argue with the Referee – is an exercise in futility. Though it would be presumptuous for me to speak about the decisions and decrees of our Creator/Referee, it is clear that

G-d sees things from many more perspectives and from countless different angles than mortal man can. What to us may appear unjust and unreasonable is surely correct and appropriate when viewed from the angles of eternity and omniscience. Therefore, investing our energies and emotions in attempting to reverse the decision of the Referee is a misdirection of resources.

Life should not be a series of complaints that one "could have" or "should have," nor should it be a daydream about "if only…" Rather, life can be immeasurably enriched by one's positive approach in times of stress and crisis. "Now, what do I do?" "How do I proceed?" and "Let us now regroup and move ahead" are coping statements which set us on the path to spiritual and mental health. The past is gone and irretrievable. The future is not yet here. It is only the fleeting present that we can deal with. All great teams and individual champions know this and win no matter what the referee's call. They go out and play harder and smarter, and do not repeat past mistakes. We should do the same. Repentance, new attitudes, corrected behavior, all make a great impression on the Eternal Referee. New insight and renewed personal efforts, not arguments and curses, are the correct responses to life's calls. Even in reference to a human referee our sages taught: "Woe is to the generation that judged its judges." We can infer that this surely applies a million times over concerning the Ultimate Judge.

Survival Tactics

One deadly foe of all creativity and progress – technological, political, economic, social and spiritual – is habit. Habit soon becomes rote and rote numbs our senses as far as invention and freshness are concerned. Individuals and societies that are frozen in the past are doomed to become relics, museum artifacts, extinct creatures. Ingenuity is the partner of imagination, two great gifts from G-d that make humankind special. G-d has, so to speak, revealed Himself to us through Creation – through that Divine imagination that fills our universe and touches all of our senses. We, by using our imagination, enrich our lives and color an otherwise drab reality. Through our imagination and creativity we are able to renew ourselves, recharge our enthusiasm for life itself, and grow and change.

Make a commitment to do something new every day,

to read, to study, to observe nature and people, to think, to plan and to dream. Even after over four decades in the kitchen, my wife, who is truly a gourmet cook, is always ready to search for, and work with, new and exciting recipes. (I knew I had a winner when after only a week of married life she cooked up a dish called "banana fritters" for me!) Imagine finding yourself in faraway places or undertaking trips to exotic destinations. Envision eternity, internalize ultimate fulfillment. Don't give in to habit and rote. Do something as prosaic as taking a different route to the office, or stimulate your brain by forcing yourself to think about an old problem in a new way.

A friend of mine is a survivor of Auschwitz. At times, he would talk to me and unburden himself about that terrible place and time. Once, in an unguarded moment of discussion, I asked him to what he attributed his survival since all of his bunkmates, many physically far stronger than he, had died. After making proper acknowledgment of the hand of Providence, he told me the following: "In 1932, as a young, well-to-do businessman from Budapest, I went on a trip to the Holy Land. I was so enamored of the country that I bought a house in Jerusalem on the spur of the moment. I usually never allowed my emotions to rule my behavior, let alone my wallet, but this time I acted impulsively and out of character. The house was badly in need of refurbishing, so I hired an architect to draw up the necessary plans to redesign and rebuild the dwelling. I then became absorbed in other business projects, and I never actually had time to follow up on the plans or the renovation. However, every night in Auschwitz, while lying together with 13 other human beings on a plank of wood that was the width of a king-size bed, after a day of labor and humiliation, pain and death, with my senses numbed by hunger, lice and filth, I imagined how I was going to rebuild that Jerusalem apartment of mine. I furnished and refurnished it every night in my imagination. I moved walls and opened windows, and every night I imagined it differently. That is how I survived those 10 months in Auschwitz. That is how I saved my sanity and my Jewish faith."

Ingenuity and imagination equip us to survive reality, no matter how awful. The power of self-renewal is fueled by fresh approaches and imaginative insights. Not everything new will work for us, but humans cannot work successfully without being constantly refreshed and challenged by the new and the ingeniously imaginative. We should consciously re-evaluate our dreams and aspirations, always searching for new ways to improve ourselves. Such use of our creative and imaginative skills will help us through difficult times.

But it is Sooo Boooring

The most dreaded words that can issue from a child's mouth are, "It is so boring." A child's attention span is notoriously short. The $35 game that we bought for him just today is already "boring" tomorrow. This childish trait remains with many of us even as we age and mature. There are those of us who become restless and easily bored. We are always searching for the new and exciting, and everyday living itself can then seem to be tedious. Our marriages, families, careers and lifestyles can all very easily be invaded by the dreaded specters of sameness, habit, and boredom. Thus our entire joy of living and our very reason for being become threatened.

Many people who have worked their entire life, and retire while still physically active and in good health, are often overcome with boredom. Psychologists have noted that this type of boredom can lead to deteriorating health and mental depression. Every person must adjust early in life to the realization that much in life, even – or perhaps especially – the good things in life, might appear, on the surface, to be essentially boring. A stable marriage, a loving family, good health, a fulfilling job and financial security, might seem to some to be inherently boring. And yet, this is a fallacy that seems true only because of our mistaken attitudes and our distorted view of life. Secure, stable, worthwhile and solid are words that should not imply even a hint of boredom. Rather, as we thoughtfully examine the priceless gifts that we have been granted by our Creator and as we really appreciate them, we can learn to realize that life acquires an inner rhythm and excitement of its own. This is what truly makes each day and each experience different and challenging.

Taking things for granted is what makes life boring. Realizing how fragile and temporary we really are automatically lends interest and challenge to even oft-repeated facets of our lives. Many people have discovered that regular meaningful prayer is an excellent example of how we can learn to be more conscious of our own special uniqueness. In addition, prayer grants us the opportunity to create for ourselves, on a daily basis, a meaningful new world of spiritual exploration and intellectual growth. This is certainly a recipe designed to banish boredom! As we take time to stop and smell the roses and appreciate the beauty of G-d's world, our souls receive nourishment and our spirits become serene, and the joy we receive from the "little things" can aid in providing us with the priceless gifts of physical and mental health.

I once recommended a trip to the Grand Canyon to a friend of mine. He said, "I have already visited there a number of years ago. I am not interested in returning there again." I was shocked by his answer. I think that one can never get enough of the Grand Canyon. I would like to visit it regularly. How can one be bored by such awesome beauty? When I visited Zion National Park in Utah, I had a conversation with a park ranger who has worked at that Eden for decades. He told me: "I have asked for permission to continue to give tours here at Zion even after my retirement. I see some new wonder here every day." There are many places, such as the Grand Canyon and Zion Park, where G-d's artistic talent is constantly on display for our wonder and awe. The truth is that each and every new day provides us with the unique opportunity to see even the familiar from a fresh and elevating perspective.

There is nothing certain in our lives, and that knowledge alone should stimulate our sensitivity to the glory of G-d's world. In the Book of Psalms it is written, "How great are Your works, G-d. You made them all with wisdom, the world is full of Your possessions." In our daily prayers we add, "In His goodness, He renews daily, perpetually, the work of Creation." Look around and see the things and sights that have always been there but that you have not as yet noticed. Explore and discover on an ongoing basis. Read and study regularly. Learn something new each day. Take courses and develop new interests in your life. There is truly no necessity for boredom, except for that which is, unfortunately, self-inflicted.

Quitters Ultimately Are Losers

There are many moments in life when we are sorely tempted to quit. People regularly and, in fact, in overwhelming numbers, quit on their marriages, their children, their parents, their careers. Lately it has become fashionable to quit even on life itself.

Quitting is not really an appropriate choice in most life decisions. Understandably, there are marriages that should end; there are children and parents from whom one must perforce distance oneself; there are bad career choices that should be terminated. However, these are all last resorts, to be put into action after all else has been tried and has failed. The worst sin of all, the greatest tragedy in life, is to quit on oneself. We all have handicaps, weaknesses, fears and moments of despair. The true test of the human spirit, of the G-dly spark that lives within every human being, is his or her tenacity and determination to persevere, to succeed and to overcome. King Solomon, in Proverbs, teaches us that "The righteous shall fall seven times, but yet rise." We all fall, even the most righteous of men, but what makes a person truly "righteous" is the ability to " yet rise." It is this persistence in dealing with life's problems, and the refusal to be a quitter that is the hallmark of all human achievement and success.

I have known a number of successful businessmen who have risen from the ashes of previously failed enterprises, even bankruptcies, to achieve vast financial wealth. That spirit is not limited to the financial world alone. Harry Truman suffered great financial and political reverses in his life, but his indomitable spirit was never broken. He never thought of quitting. The Army of the Potomac, under General Grant, suffered many checks and reverses at the hands of the Confederate Army of Robert E. Lee, but Grant persevered, saying, "I will fight it out on this line all summer." Ultimately, he was the one who finally forced Lee to surrender at Appomattox.

Tenacity of will is worth a battery of artillery. The gates of self-improvement are never barred, nor are the doors to repentance ever locked. There is always an opportunity to return to one's own intrinsic spiritual nature. Hope, optimism, persistence and self-discipline are the stuff of the soul and of spiritual elevation. The development of these traits puts us in touch with our true, inner self. The tradition of Judaism is that one should not give up hope even if a sharp sword is at one's throat. G-d's business, so to speak, is to deal with sinners and with those who fail, and is that not what all human beings are guilty of, at one time or another? We who have sinned or failed have to initiate contact with G-d once again and we must be persistent in His pursuit. We can never afford to be quitters, for quitters are ultimately the real losers.

Last Will and Testament

One of the most basic drives of human beings is the determination to be remembered. No one ever wishes to be forgotten or ignored, certainly not in life, and spiritually speaking, not even after death. Since our stay on earth is rather limited, we are always devising schemes, plans, methods, documents, foundations, monuments or memorials that will insure our being remembered beyond the grave, even by generations who never knew us personally.

One of the busiest areas of the legal business is all about how to transfer wealth from one generation to the next, while at the same time attempting to avoid the pitfalls of taxes, litigation, and greedy relatives. In our society of double-speak, this process has acquired the lofty name of "estate planning." Strangely enough, in the great paradox of life, the poor have less problem being remembered than the rich. I have never seen the inheritors of a relatively small estate become embroiled in the type of family feuding that often, if not usually, is the result of the carving up of the estate of a wealthy person. Money is an item of which there can never be enough. It is like drinking seawater. No matter how much you drink, it will not slake your thirst and ultimately it will kill you. I have been witness to the shouts of anger of a young bachelor brother, who was bequeathed $2 million by his father, all the while bitterly complaining because his older sister, a mother of eight, was bequeathed $3 million. "It is not fair nor right!" he declared. The poor father, who should have spent all of his money before he died, obviously is going to be remembered by his son in a way that he never anticipated or desired.

What is the best way to be remembered? In a family situation, it is by the warmth and love exhibited unconditionally to one's children and relatives. It is by the family dinners eaten together, with the computer turned off and the phone disconnected. It is by thoughtful, kind and positive conversation, by touching and soothing, by smiles and laughter and tears. In my family, the memories that bind all of our generations together are of the Sabbath and holiday tables, the Passover matzah and the

New Year honey. My grandfather, whom I remember vividly though he died when I was just 10, left us no meaningful material wealth, but rather bequeathed to us a host of spiritual gifts and memories. And amazingly enough, my own grandchildren, generations later, when they pass his picture hanging in our home, seem to also "remember" him because of shared moral and spiritual values and religious traditions which transcend time and generations, and which allow for positive and unending memory.

As far as general society is concerned, the best way to be remembered is by acts of kindness, charity, consideration and sensitivity to others. Evil people are also long remembered, but I know no one who really wants to be remembered in that way. One's last will and testament should not be restricted to a legal instrument, signed and witnessed in a lawyer's office. Every day of our lives, by our actions and attitudes, by our behavior and stated goals, we write our last will and testament and thereby determine if and how we will be remembered. In the Book of Proverbs we read, "The memory of a righteous person will bring blessing, but the name of the wicked will rot." The perpetuity that we all long for can be attained by spiritual and moral endeavors pursued while we are still alive. It follows, we trust, that our children and grandchildren will treasure this, our legacy to them, and that they will be truly blessed as they transmit that same legacy on down the line.

But I'm Not Finished!

Legend tells us that a great Renaissance artisan was commissioned to create the massive bronze doors for a huge estate home. He worked on the project for many years, always responding to the demands that he deliver the doors by saying, "But I am not as yet finished." Reaching the end of his patience, the master of the estate visited the artisan and loudly demanded to know when the doors would finally be finished. "When you come to pick them up," was the artist's reply. The truth is that in life we are never finished. We are always in the middle of something and there are always projects and activities that remain unfinished. That should not discourage us. That is simply how life is. And humans, being mortal and fallible, never achieve the perfection in their deeds or works that would truly allow the matter to be called finished. Thus, completion, closure, finishing, is always a relative matter, for nothing in this universe, even Creation itself, is ever really complete, finished or ended.

One of the more difficult realities of life which we have to accept is that when all is over we will leave behind a great deal of unfinished business. Everyone wants to leave his affairs in order and his desk neat, and justly so. But life by its very nature is a collection of loose ends and unfinished business. The perfectionist, the workaholic, the person who demands final closure on all facets of his life, whether in the area of family, business, or society, is doomed to frustration and disappointment. A great man, an outstanding scholar and philanthropist, once told me: "The secret of success, even happiness, in life is to always be in the middle of a new project, a new commitment, a new interest, a new book. That way, you are never bored or ever finished. The end of one project signals the beginning of the next. The challenge of achievement is always with you." Upon completing the payment of a major pledge to charity, he immediately undertook a new obligation that would be spread over a number of years. He told me, with a half-serious wink: "This way the L-rd will spare me for at least a number of years, for He certainly is interested in seeing that my word and pledge are redeemed!" Eighteen centuries ago, the Rabbis of the Mishnah phrased it this way: "It is not incumbent upon you to complete the tasks. But neither are you free to withdraw from those tasks during your lifetime."

There are many roles in life that always remain unfinished. One is never really finished being a parent, nor, for that matter, a child. The responsibilities and daily circumstances of these roles certainly change over the years, but the basic role itself is continuous and unending. And it is to our benefit that things remain unfinished from one generation to the next. Once again the wise words of the ancient rabbis instruct us: "Our ancestors have left over room for us to establish our mark." Every human being, every generation in our families and societies, has a contribution to make toward the betterment of the world. We build upon the unfinished accomplishments and hopes of those who have gone before us. We should therefore attempt to finish the old, begin the new, and make certain that there are worthy projects only half-done to leave to our children and grandchildren.

Berel Wein is a rabbi, lawyer, teacher, lecturer and author. His books, audio-tapes and videos on Jewish history have made him known throughout the world. He is a regular op-ed page columnist for the Jerusalem Post. He also currently teaches and lectures regularly in Jerusalem, where he and his wife live. Shaar Press published his best-selling trilogy on Jewish history, and his feature film on "Rashi" has been completed for broadcast on Israel Television.